The BROWN FAIRY BOOK

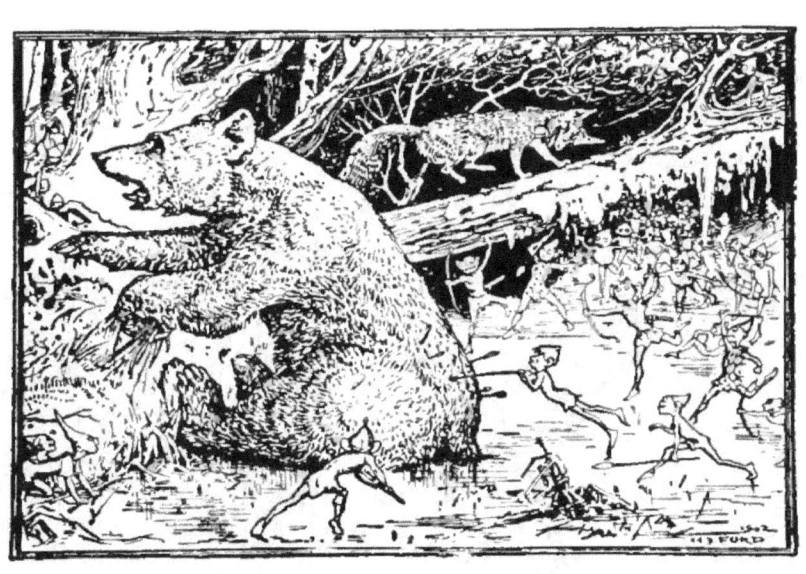

With Numerous Illustrations by H. J. Ford

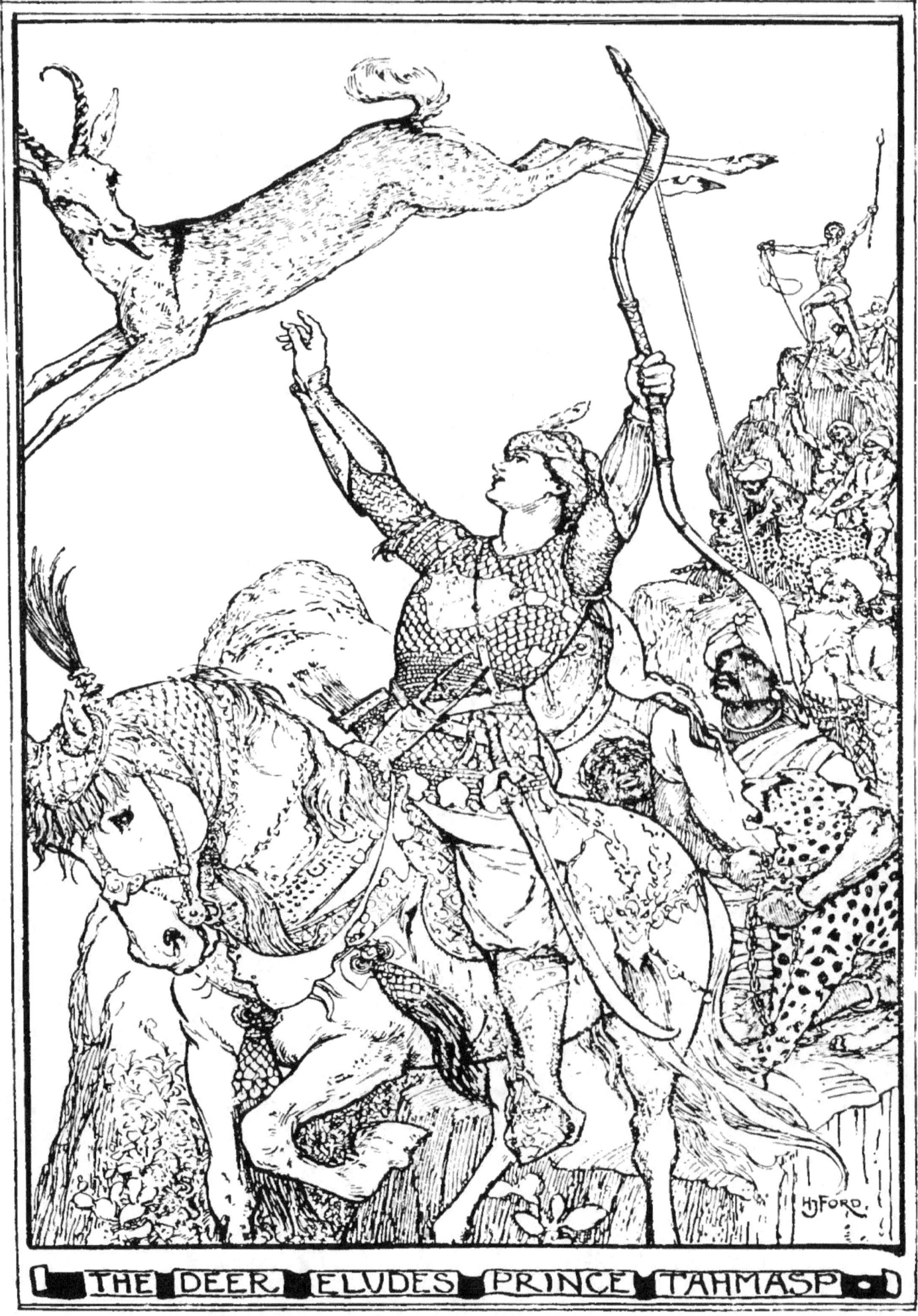
THE DEER ELUDES PRINCE TAHMASP

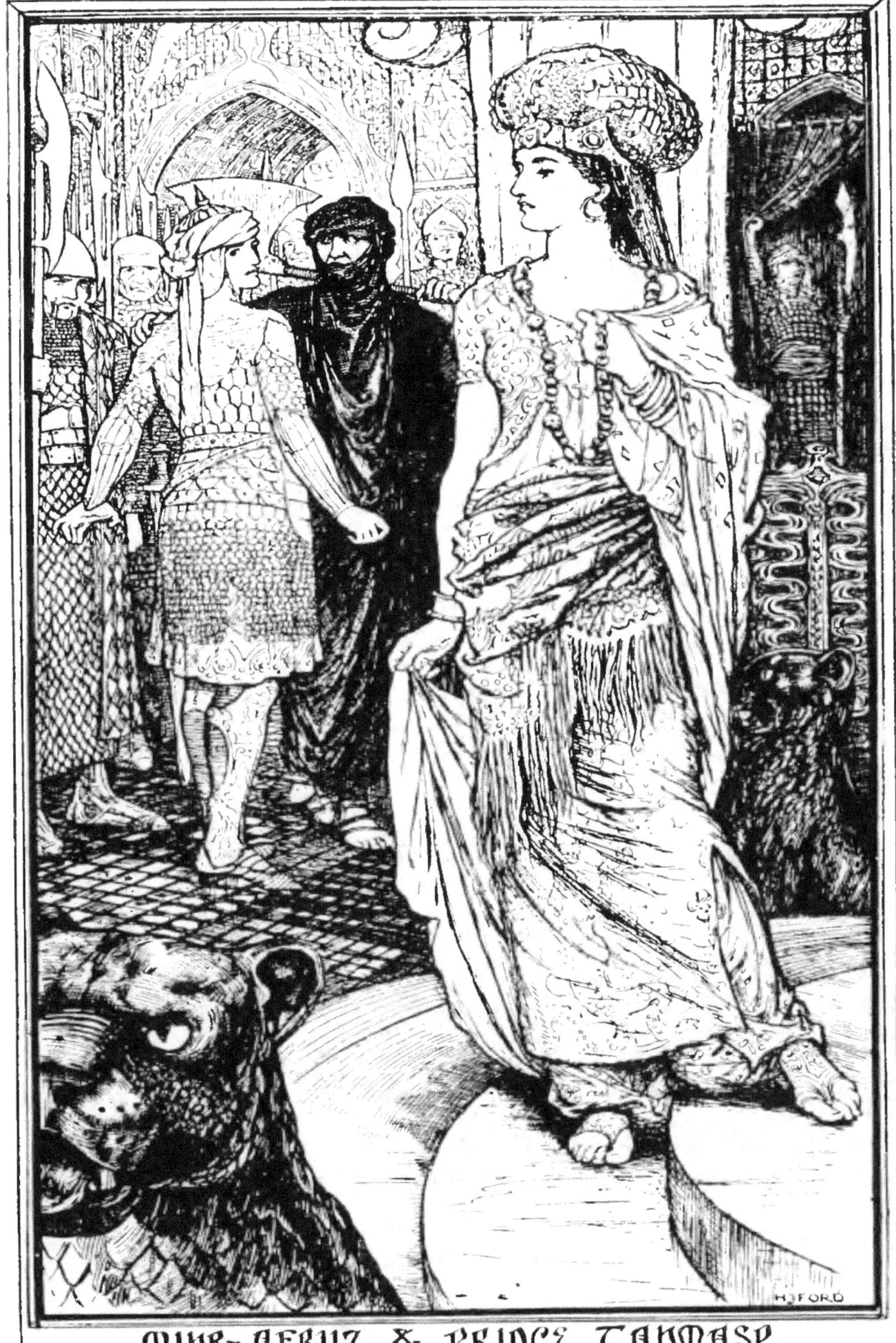
MIHR-AFRUZ & PRINCE TAHMASP

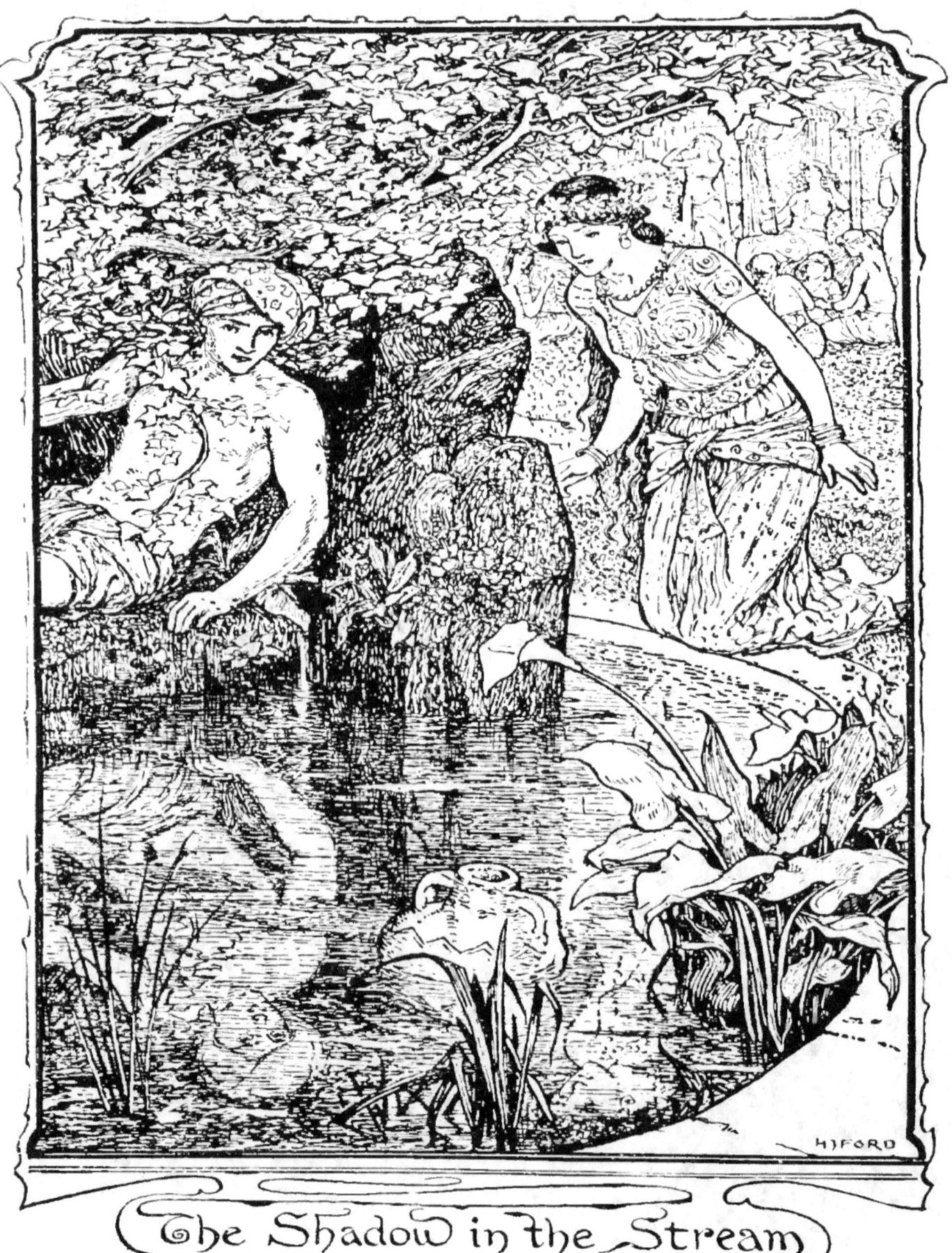

The Shadow in the Stream

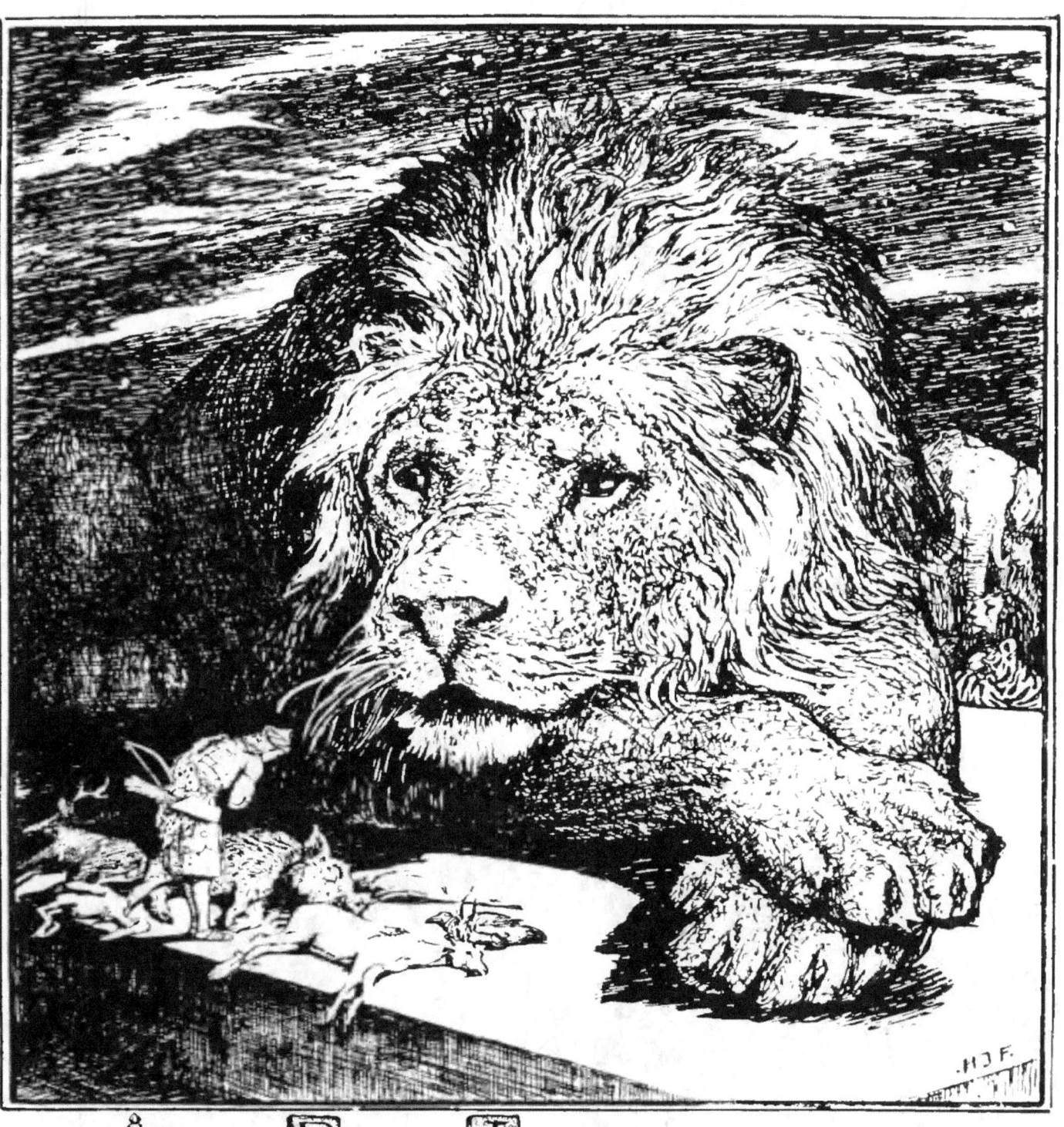

Prince Almas brings game to the King Lion

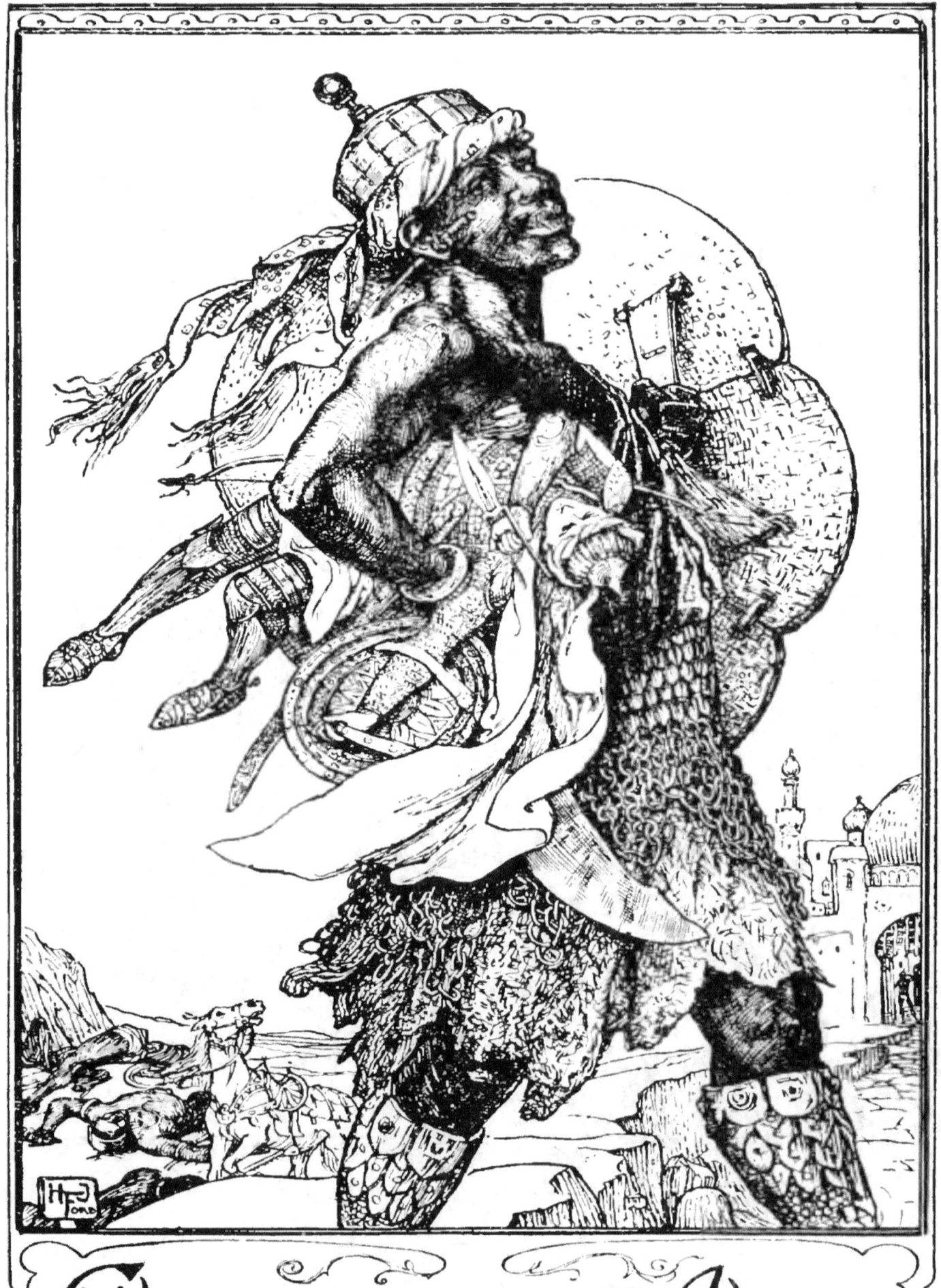

Chil-maq carries off Almas

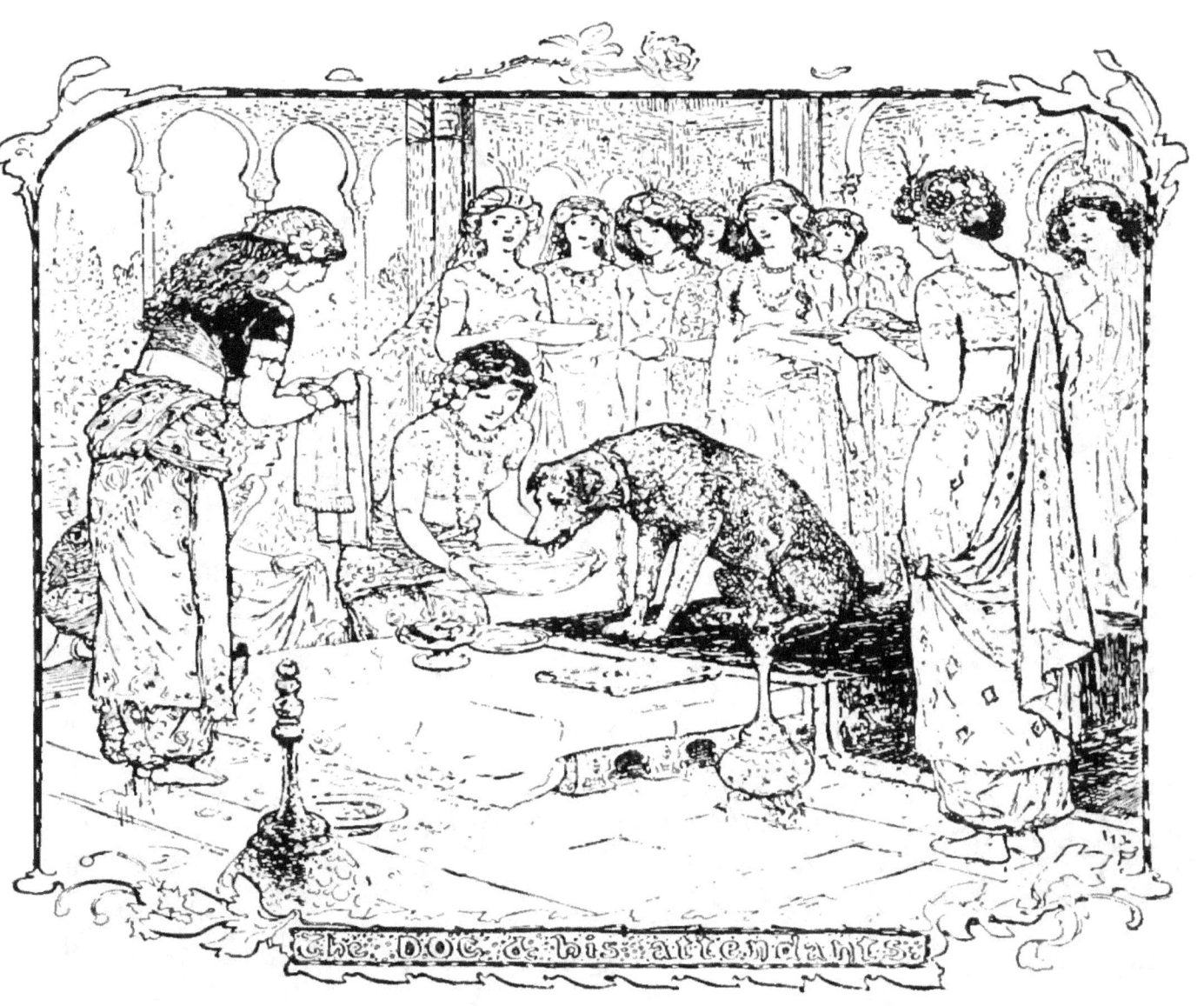
The Dog & his attendants

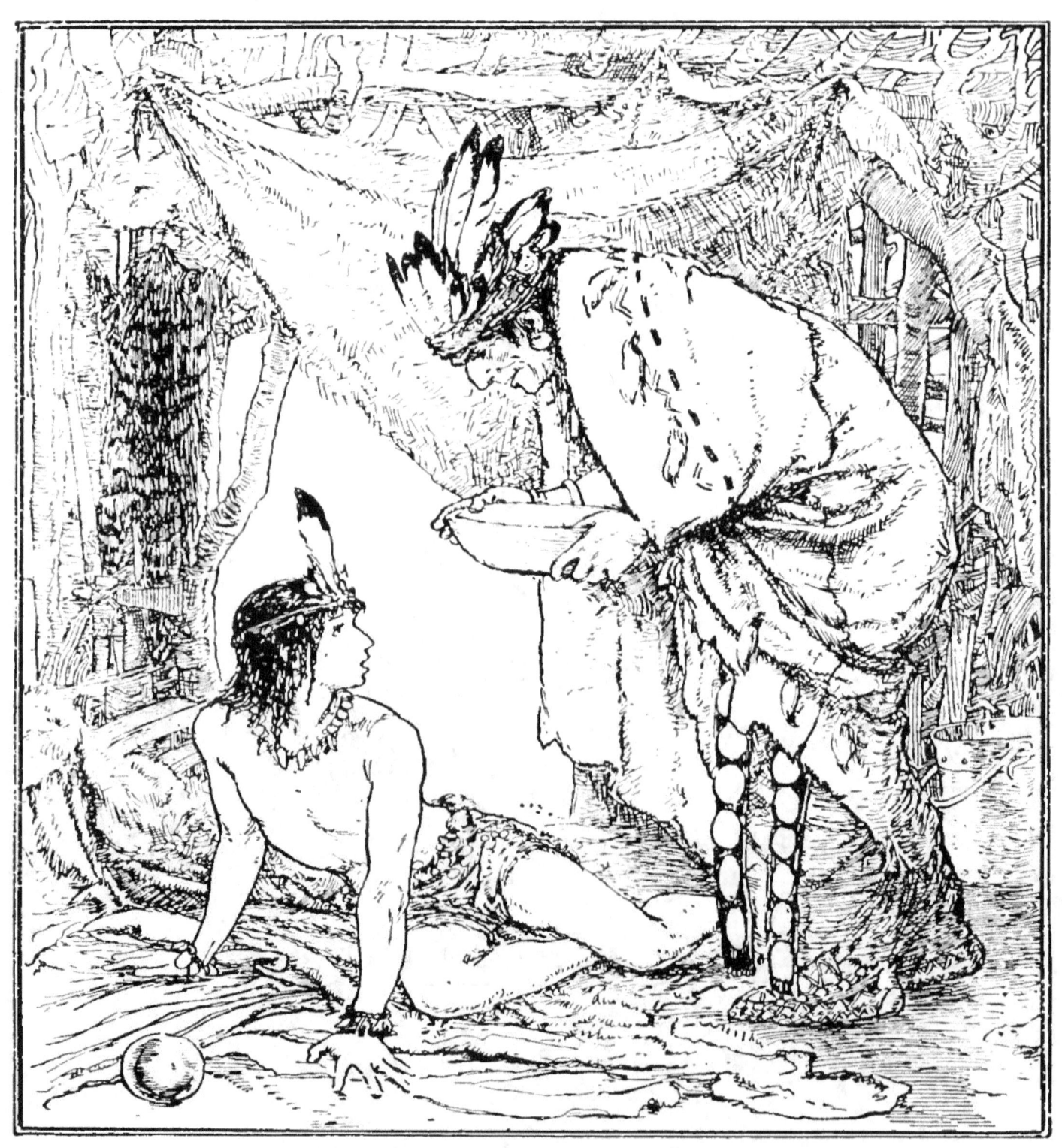
THE BOY IN THE WITCH'S HUT.

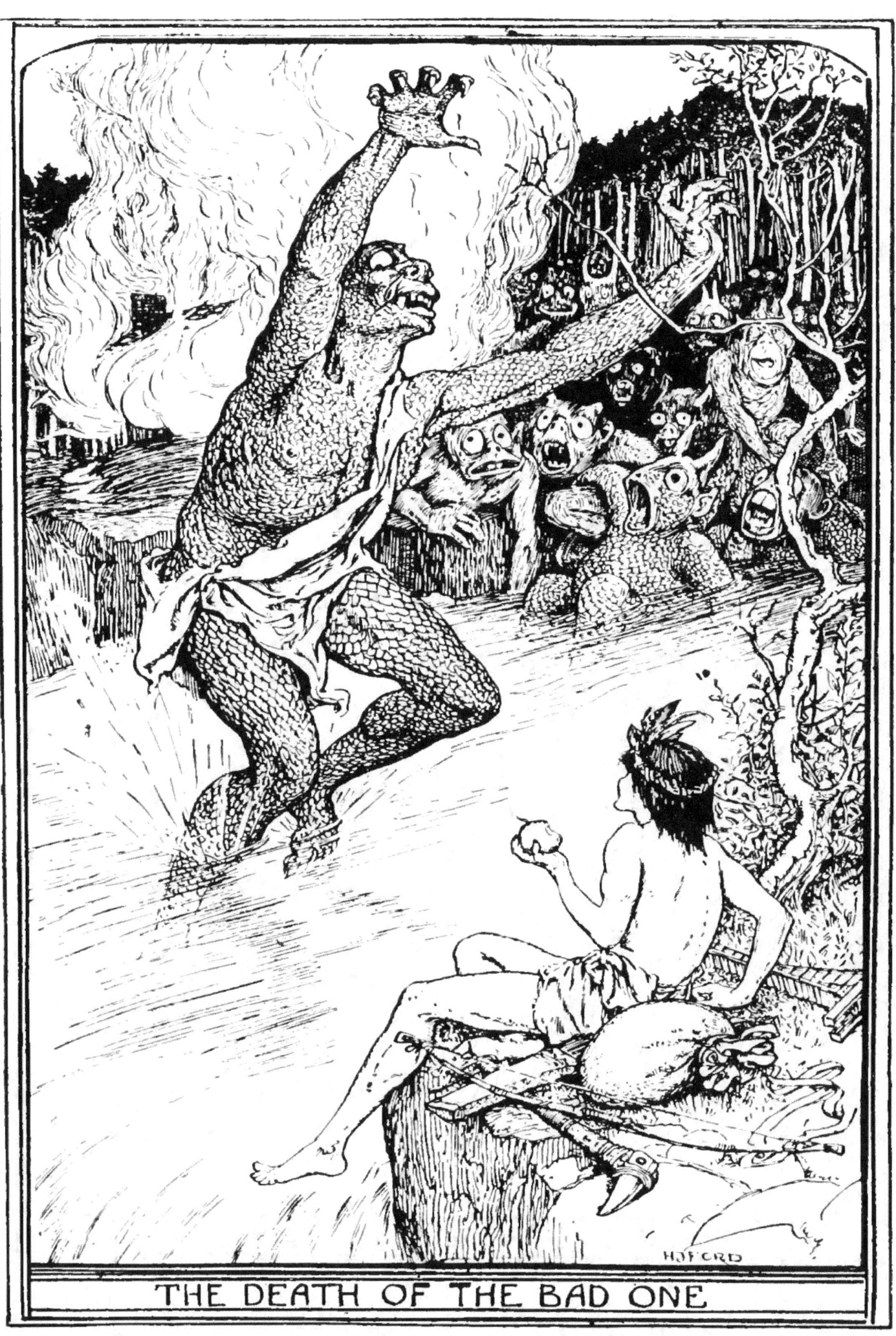
THE DEATH OF THE BAD ONE

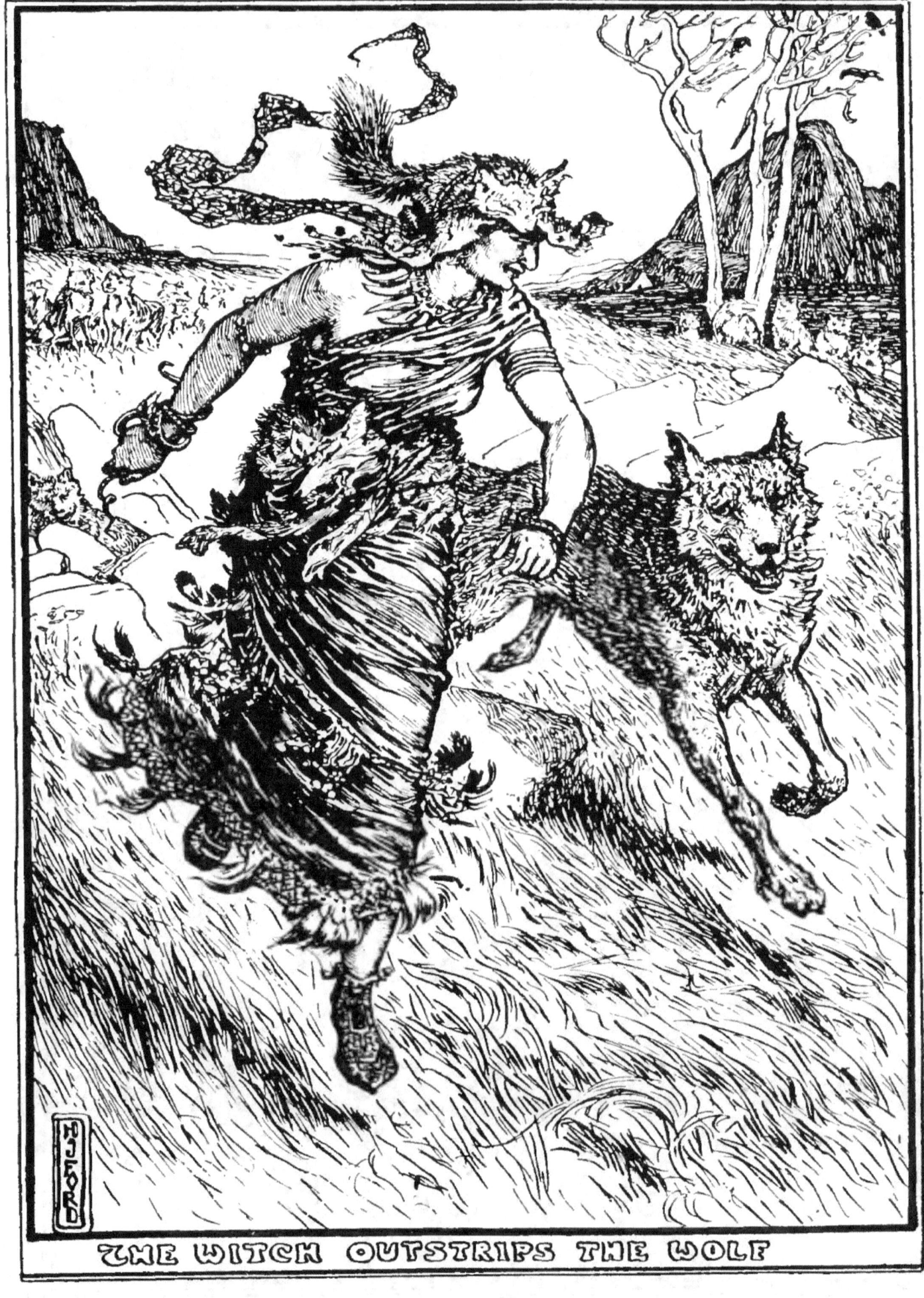
THE WITCH OUTSTRIPS THE WOLF

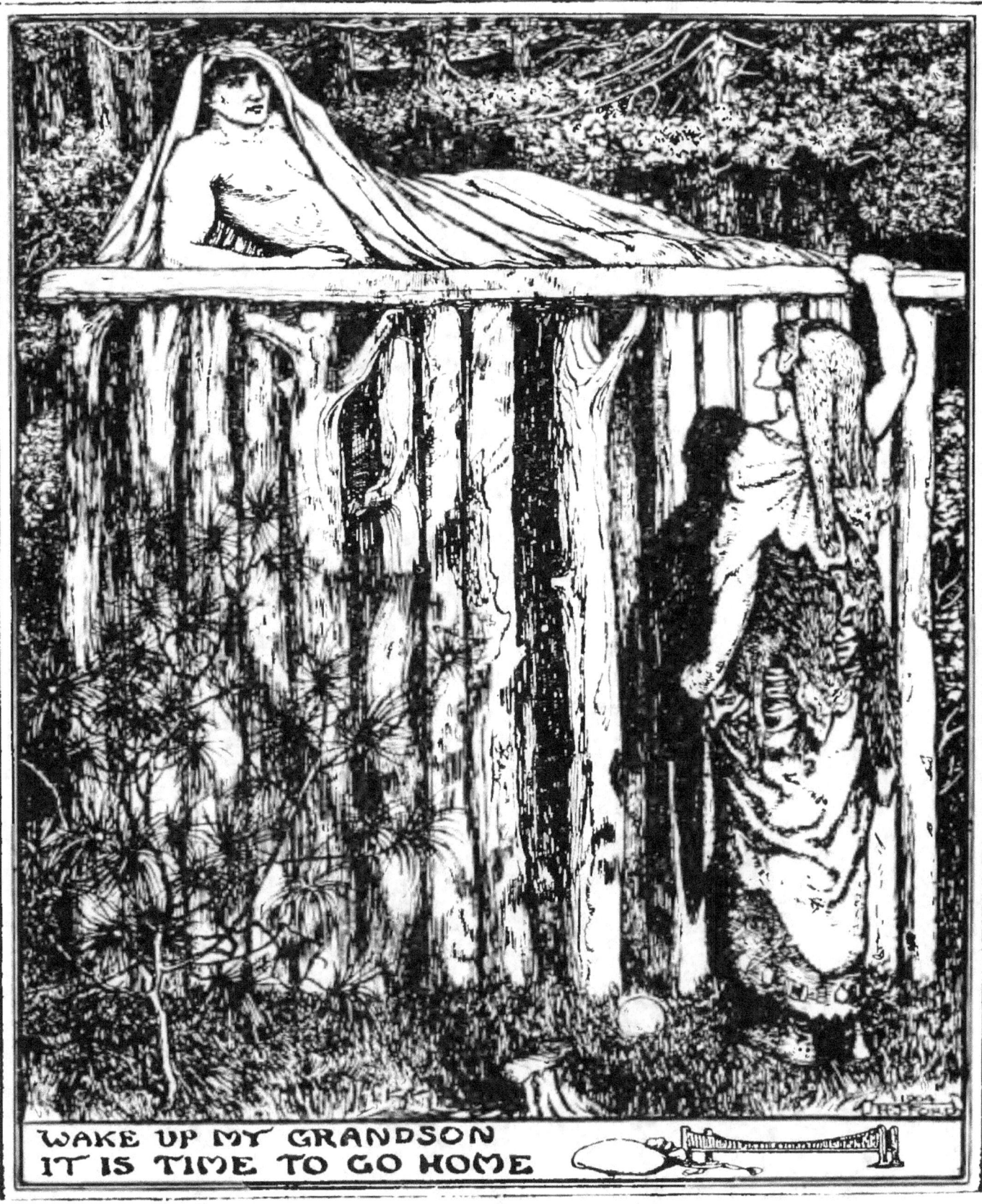
'WAKE UP MY GRANDSON IT IS TIME TO GO HOME'

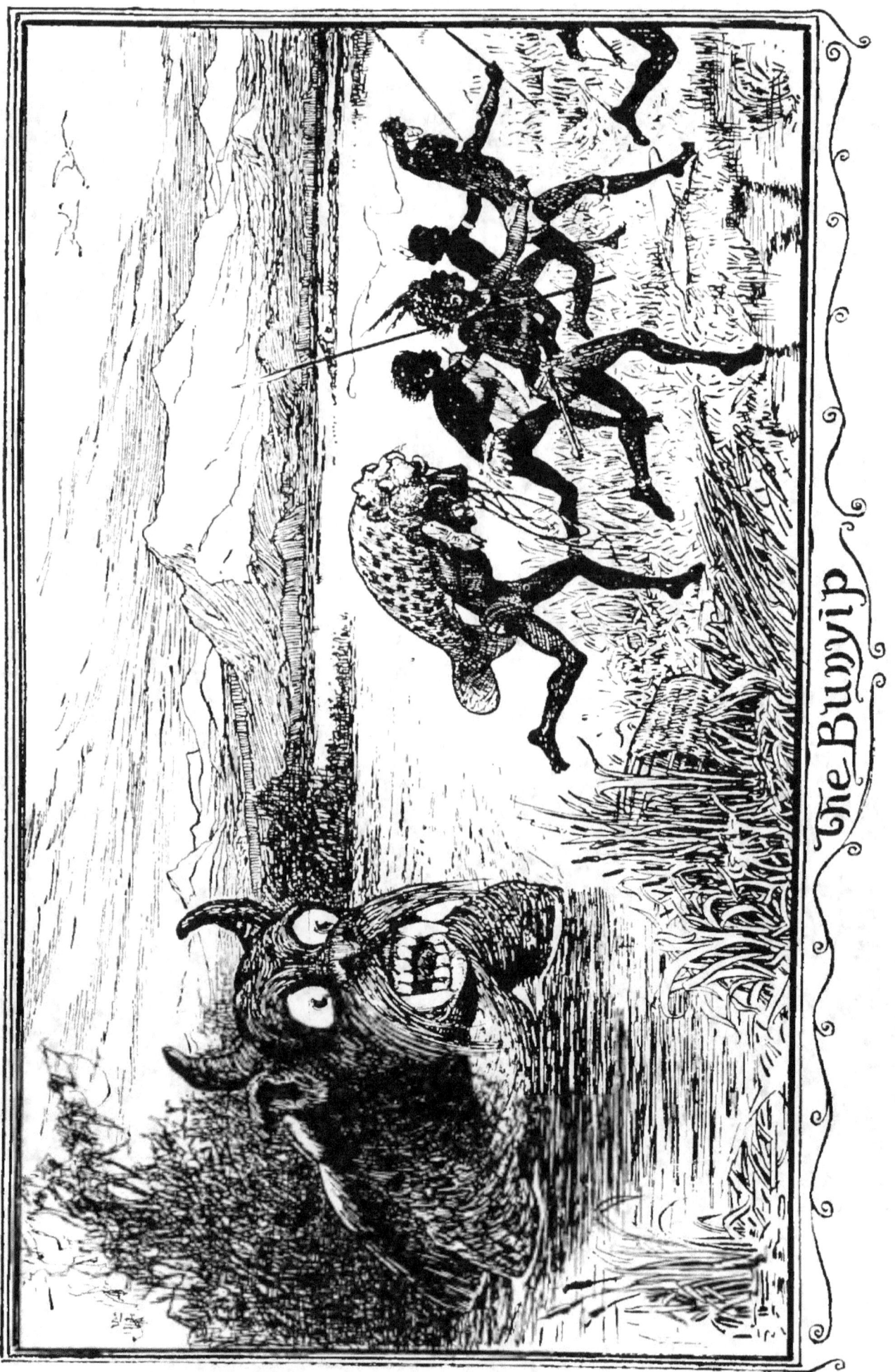

The Bunyip

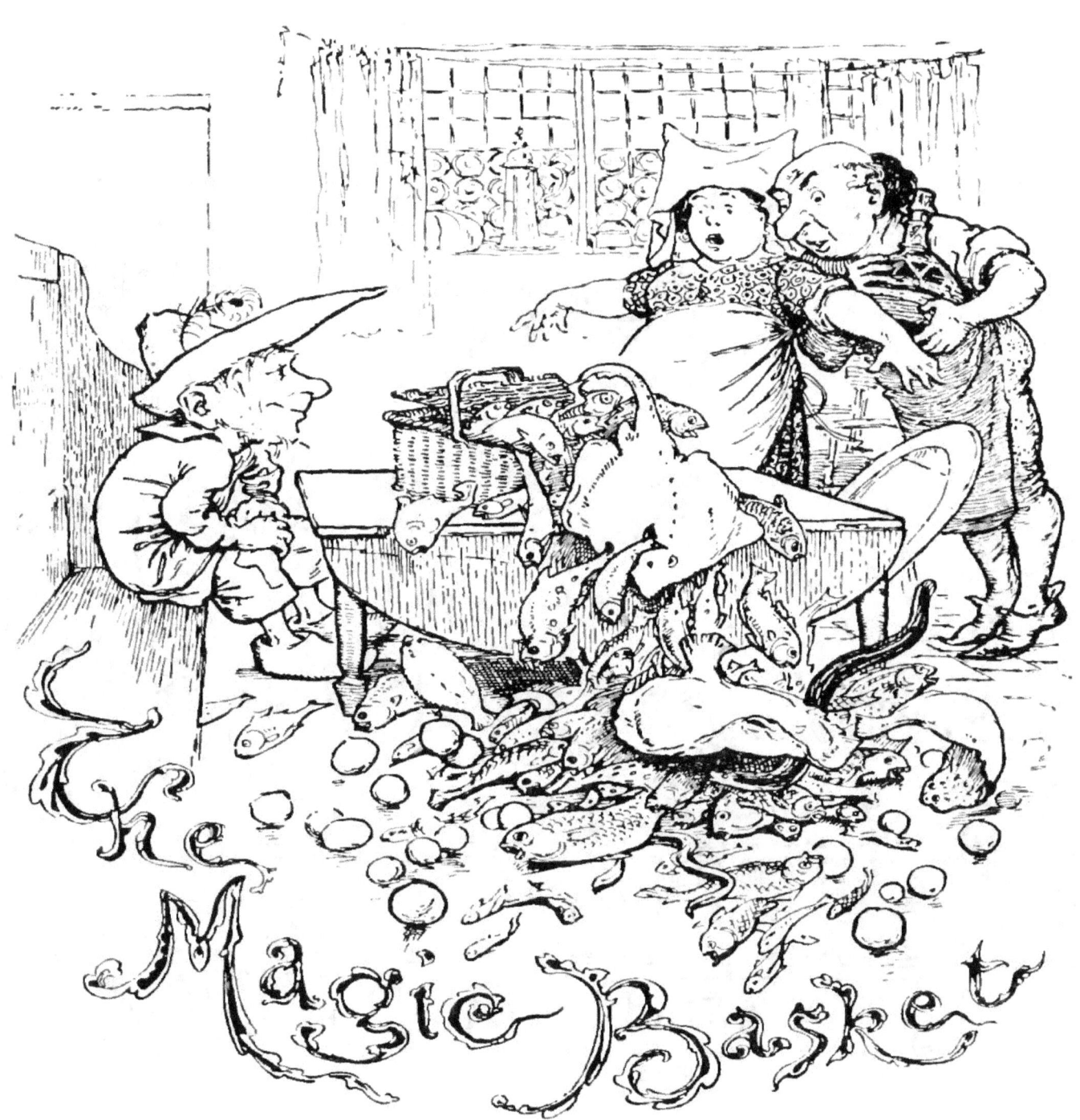

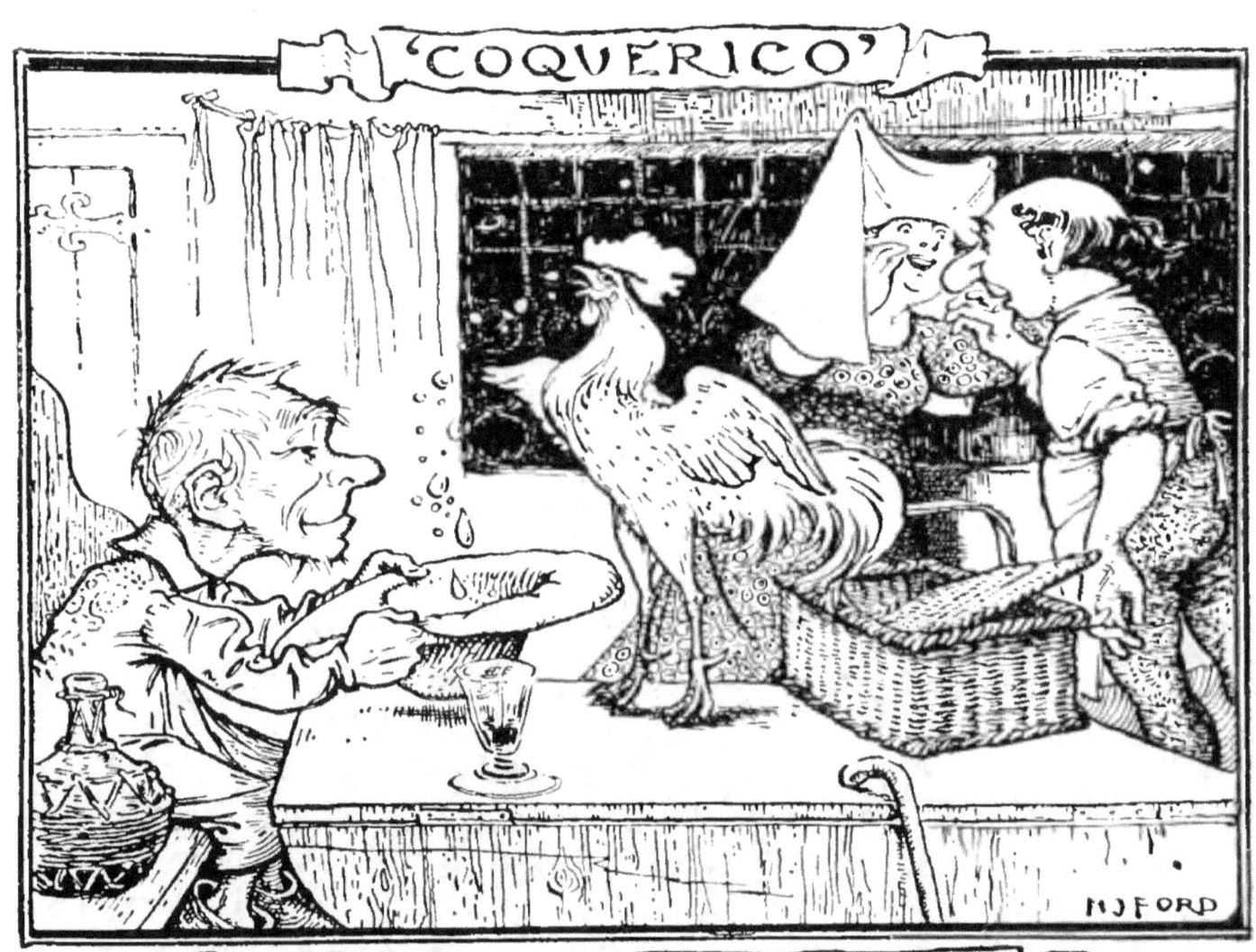

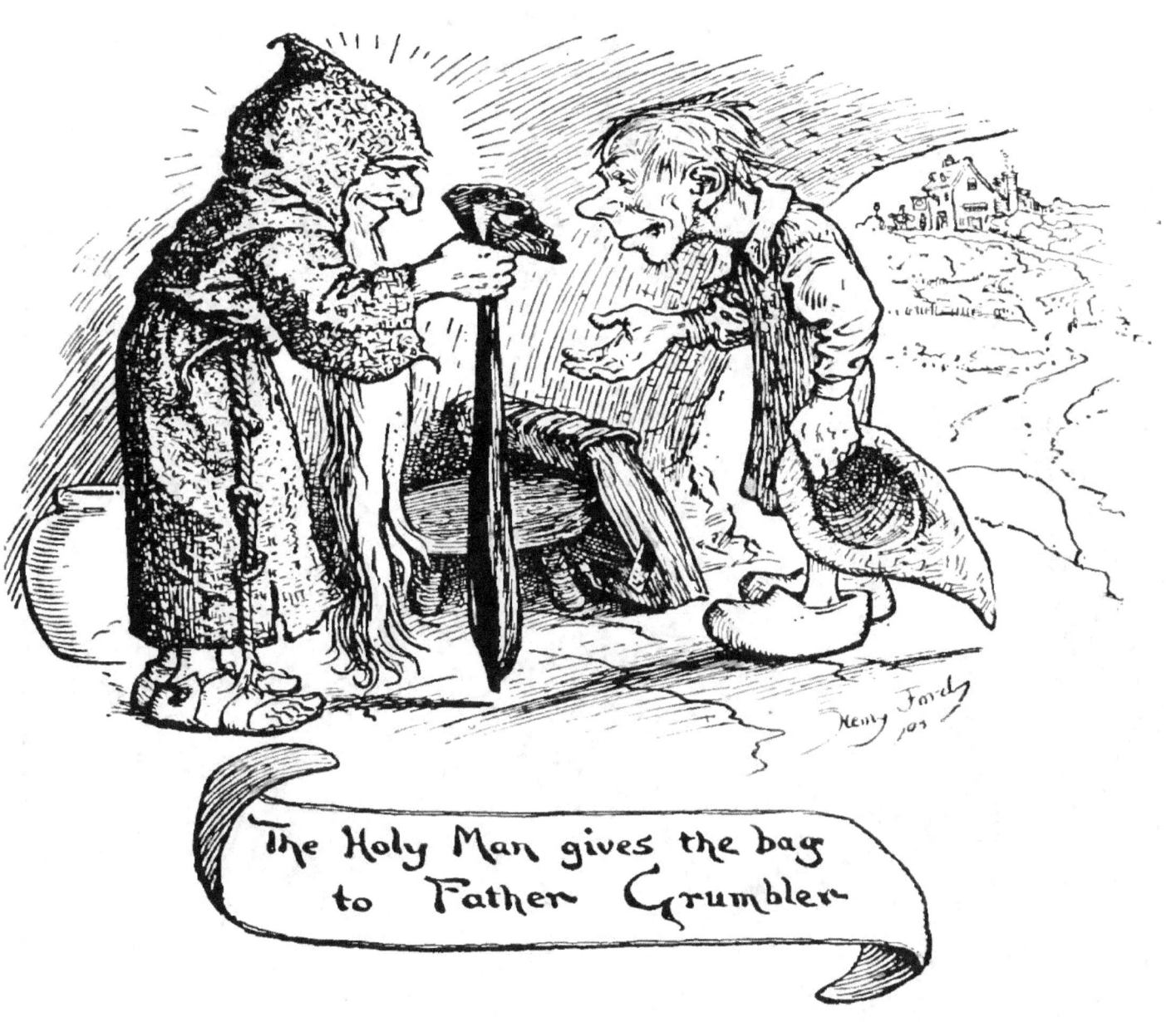

The Holy Man gives the bag to Father Grumbler

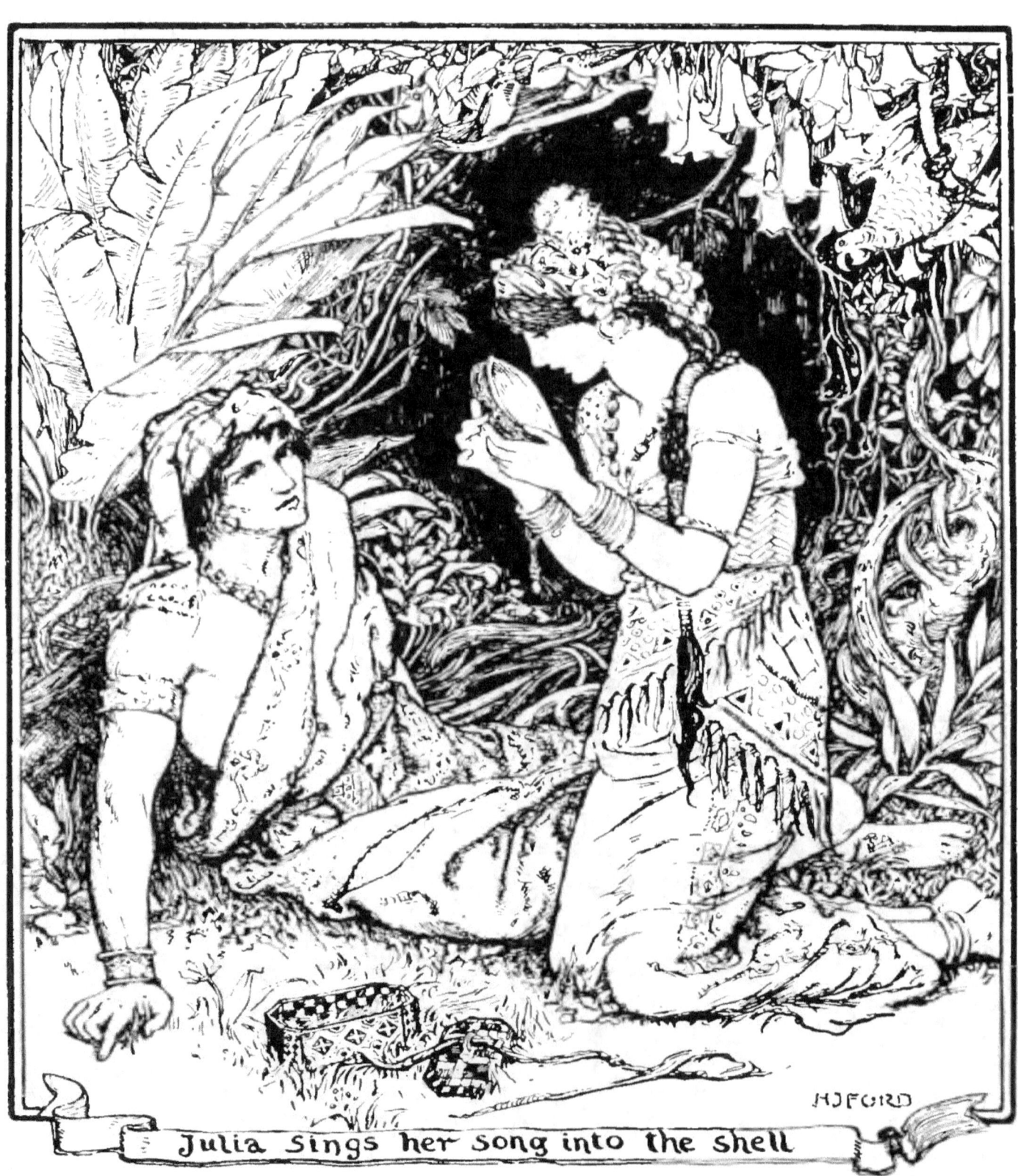
Julia sings her song into the shell

THE YARA DEFEATED

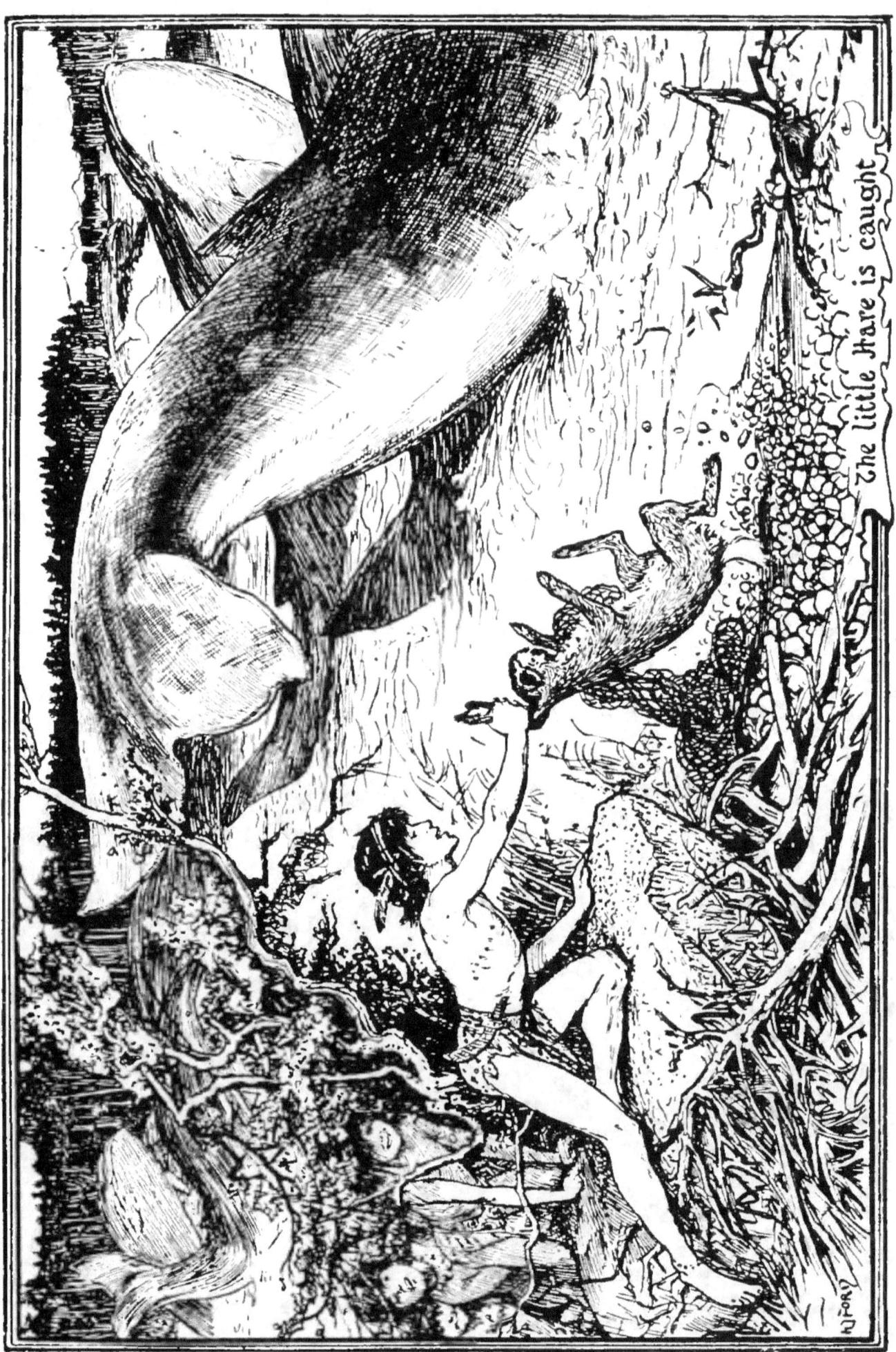
The little Hare is caught

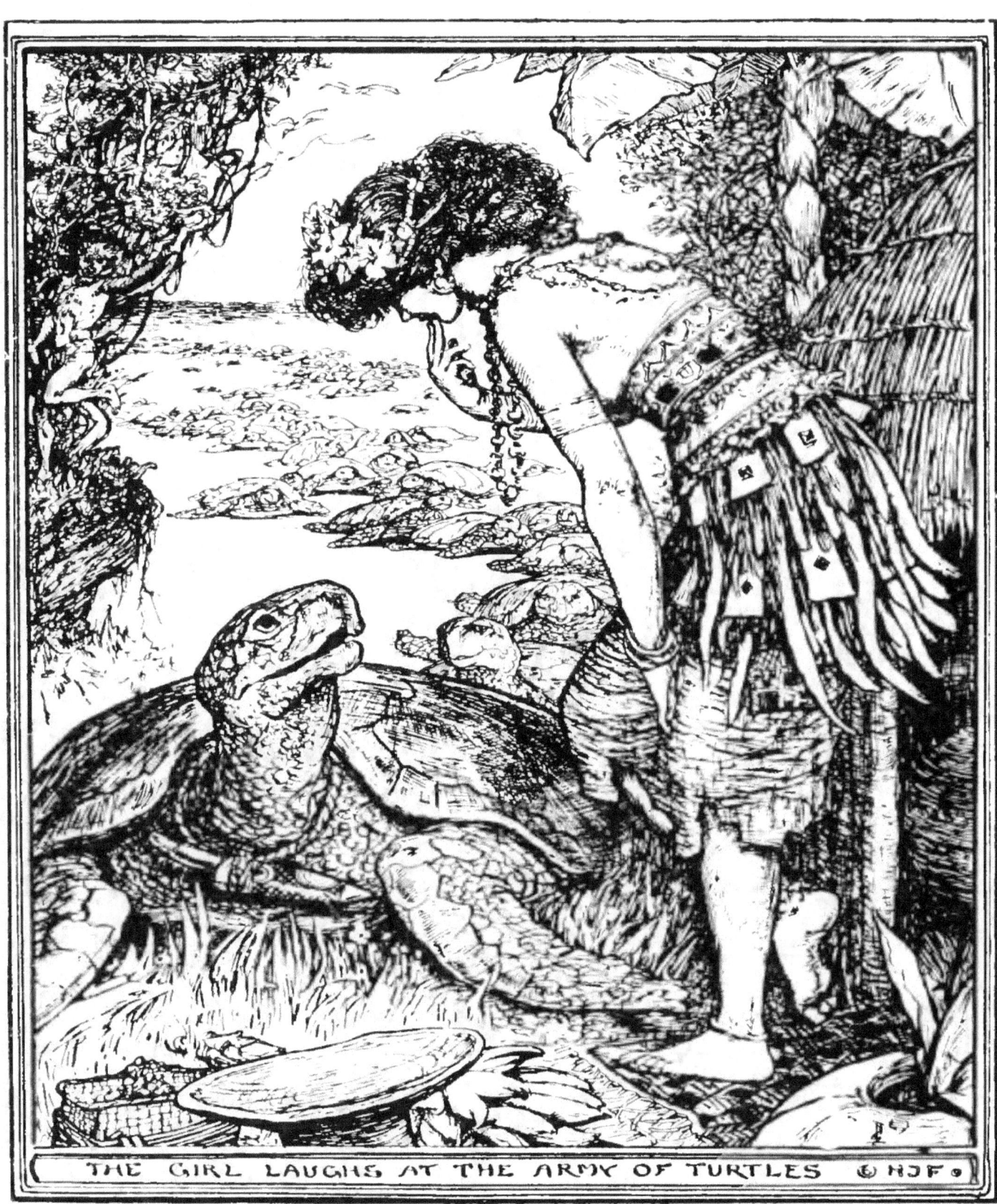
THE GIRL LAUGHS AT THE ARMY OF TURTLES

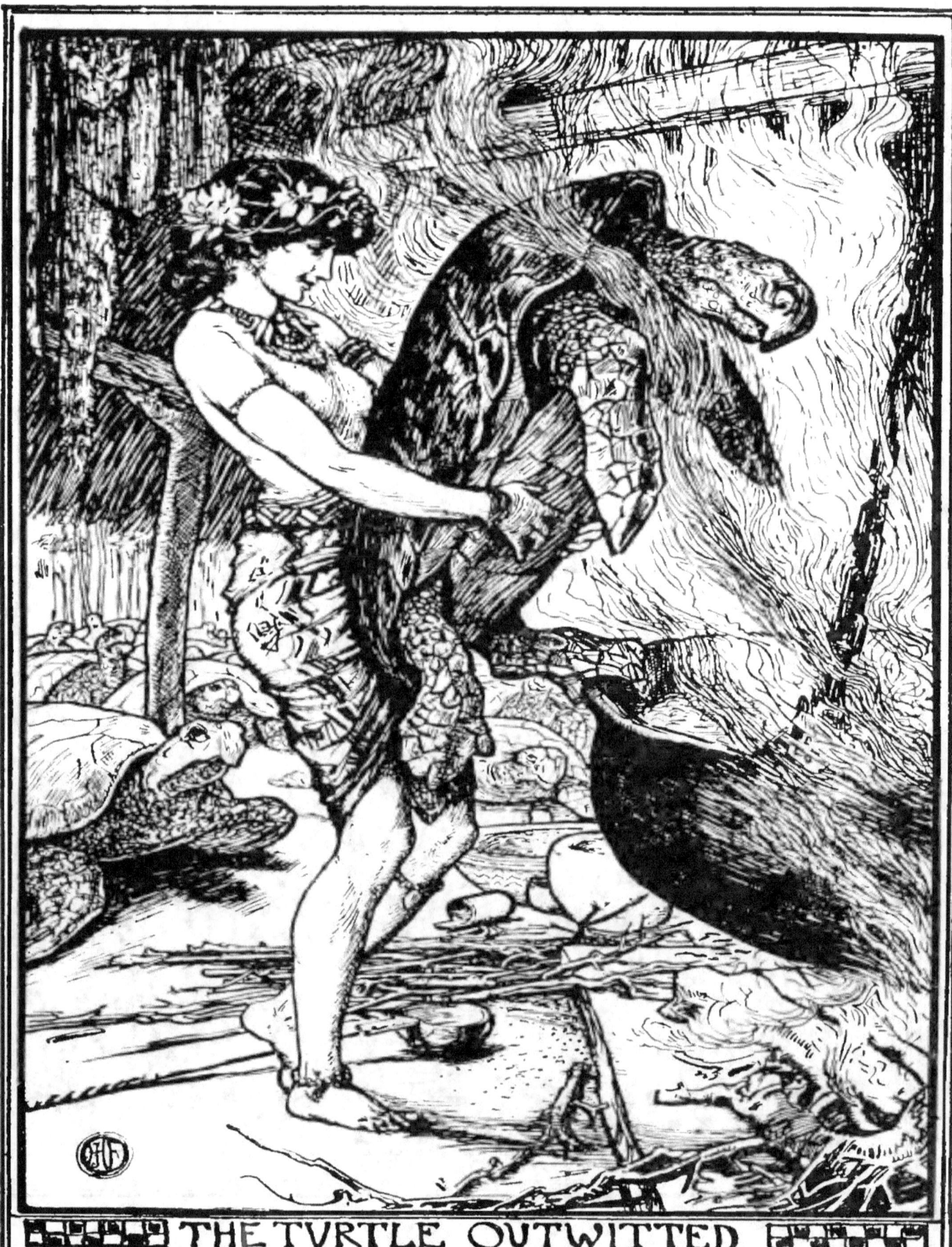
THE TURTLE OUTWITTED

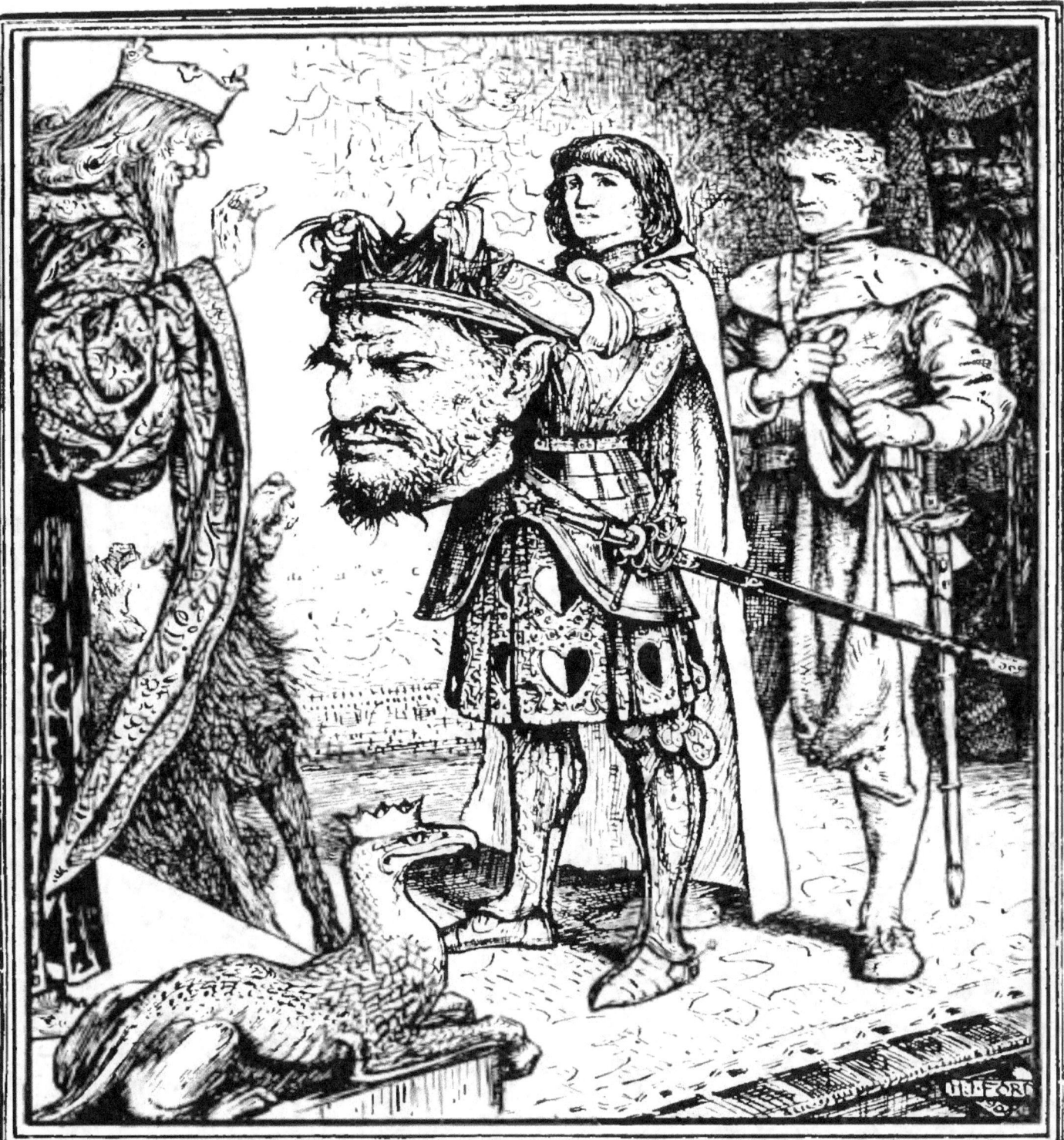

"THE GIANT WILL TROUBLE YOU NO MORE" said Geirald

—GEIRALD CLAIMS HIS REWARD AND THE QUEEN DEMANDS ANOTHER TEST—

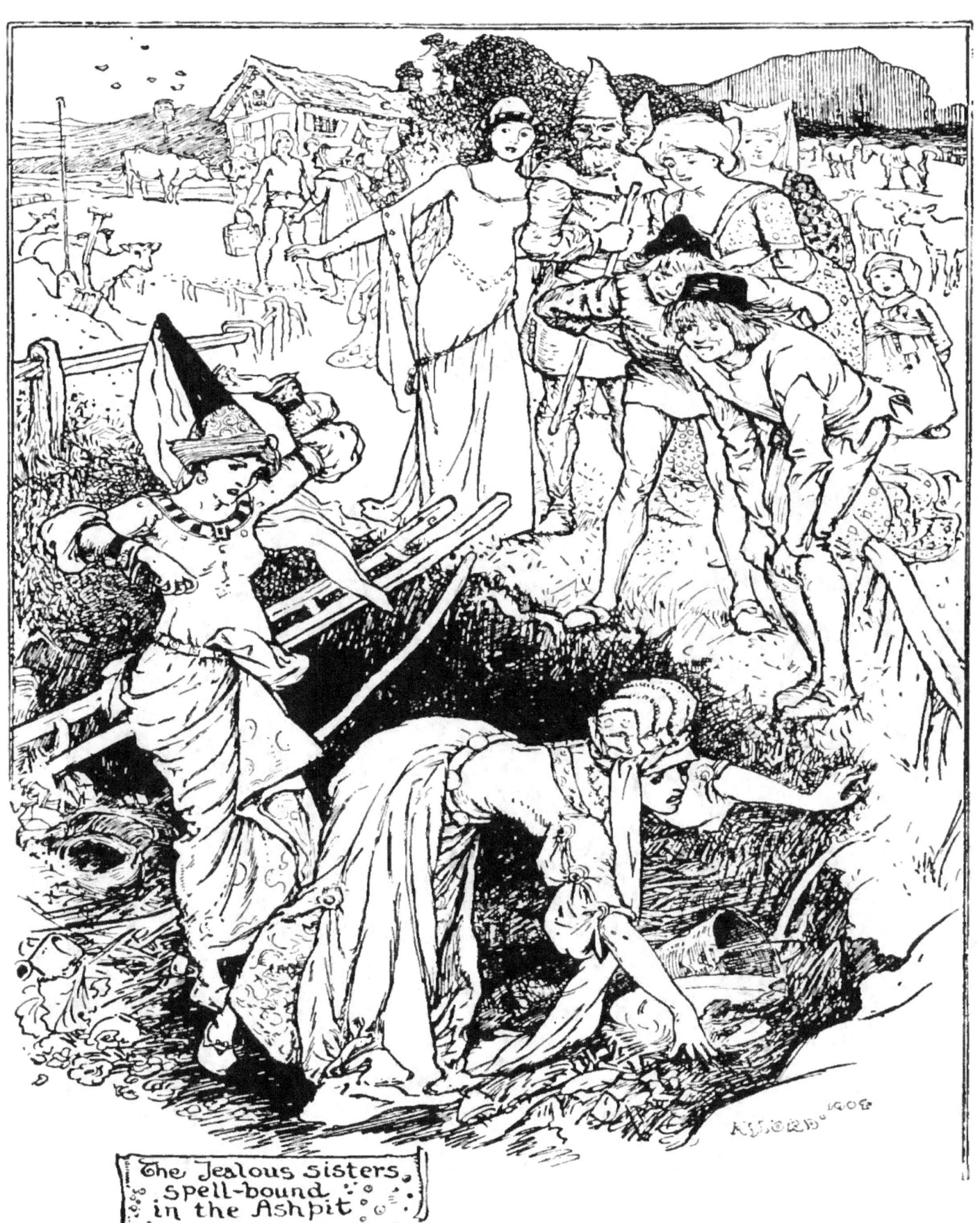

The Jealous Sisters Spell-bound in the Ashpit.

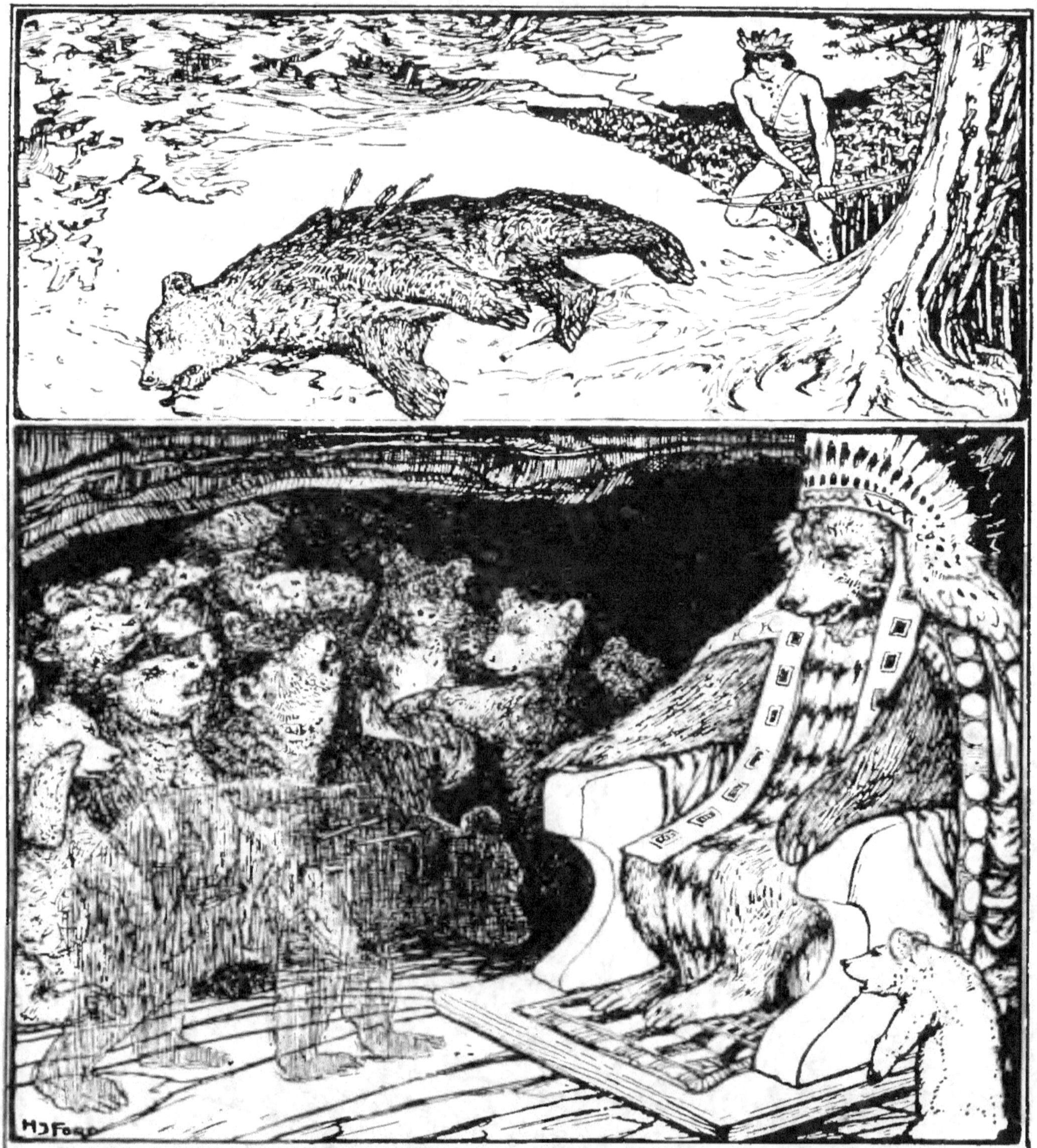

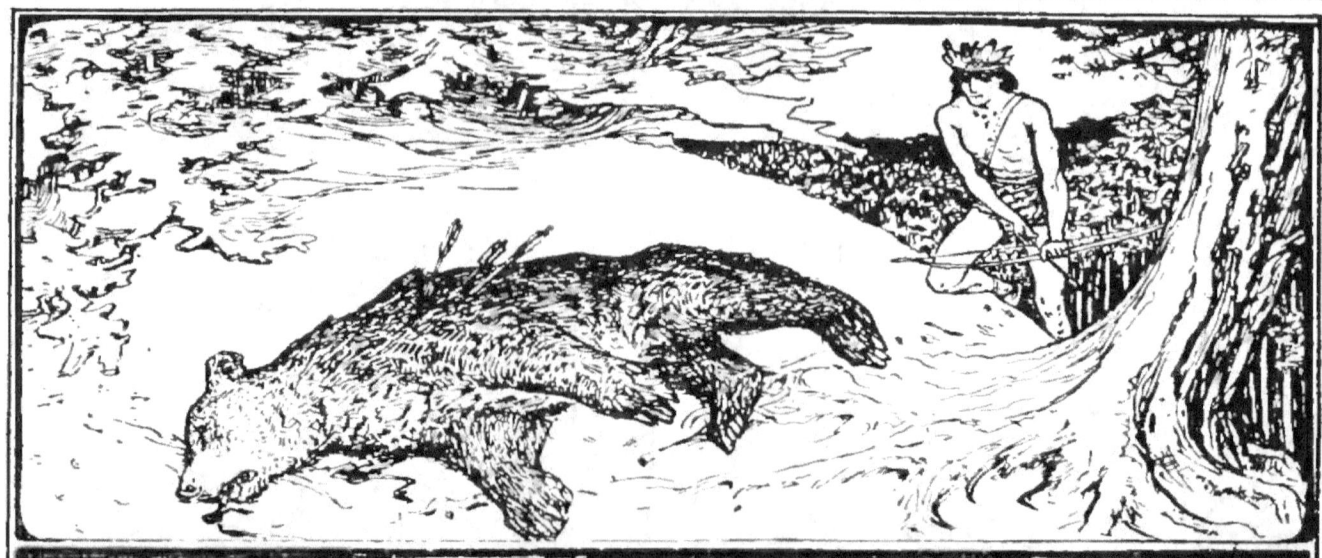

EVERY TIME A BEAR WAS KILLED HIS SHADOW RETURNED TO THE HOUSE OF THE GREAT BEAR-CHIEF

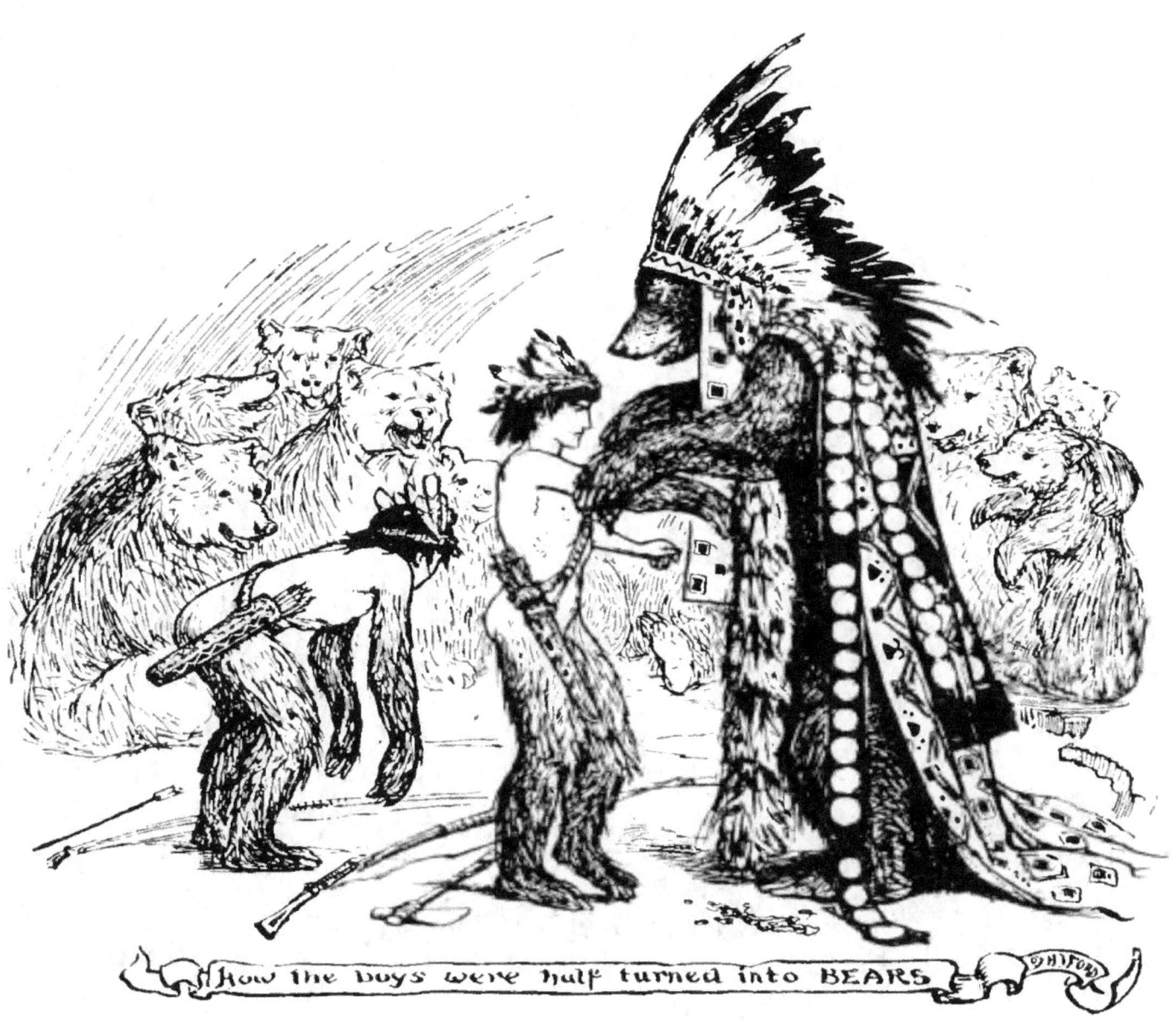
How the boys were half turned into BEARS

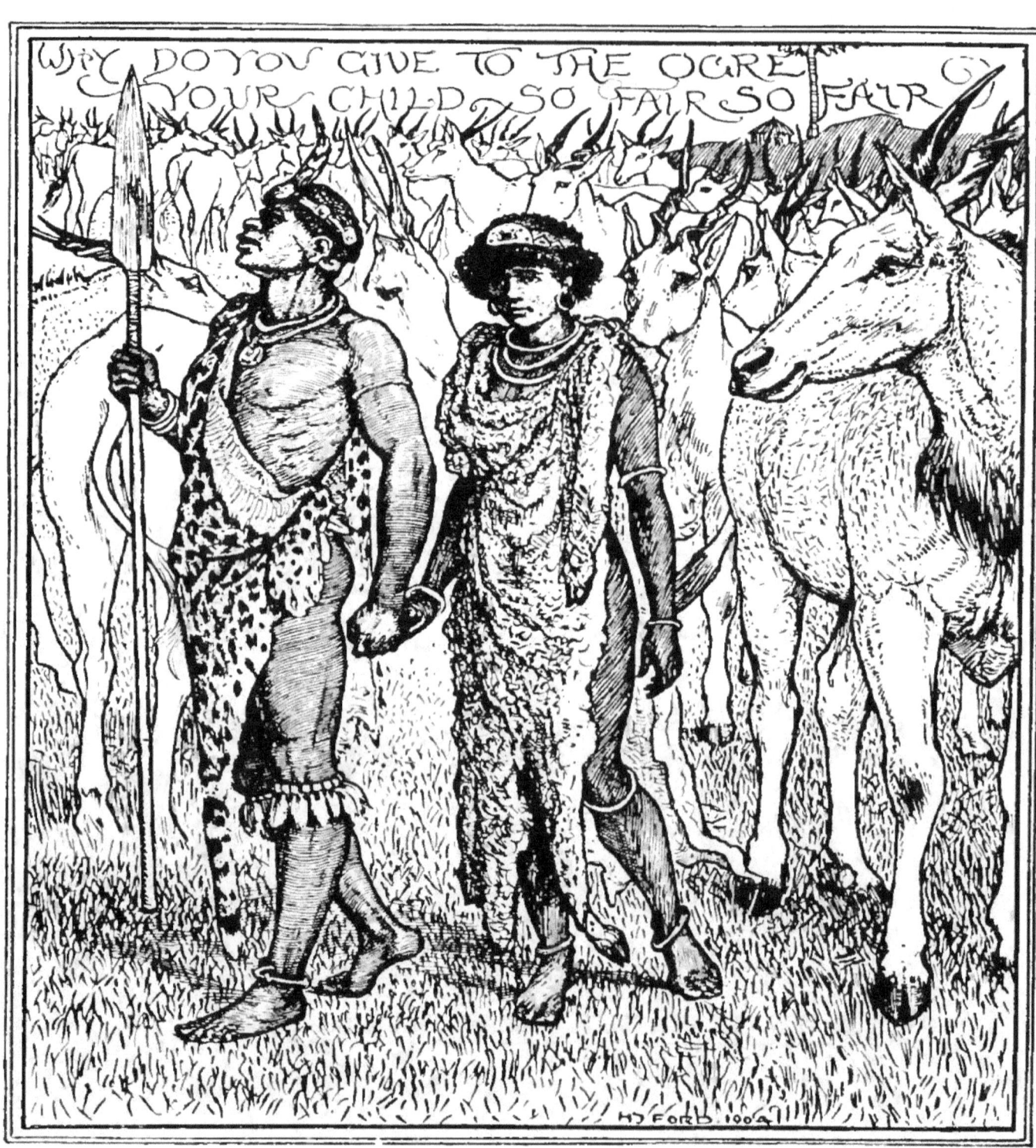

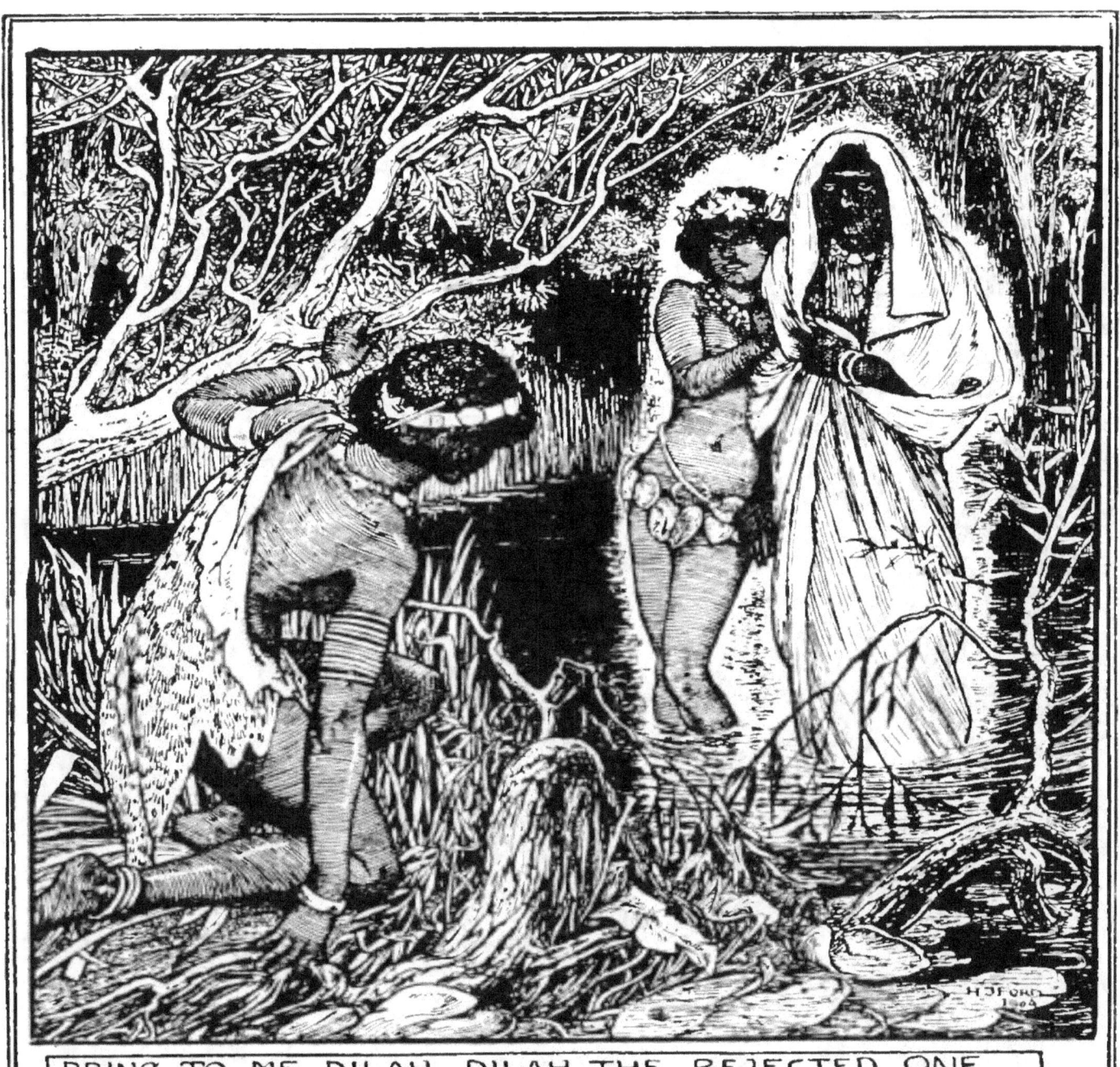
BRING TO ME DILAH DILAH THE REJECTED ONE

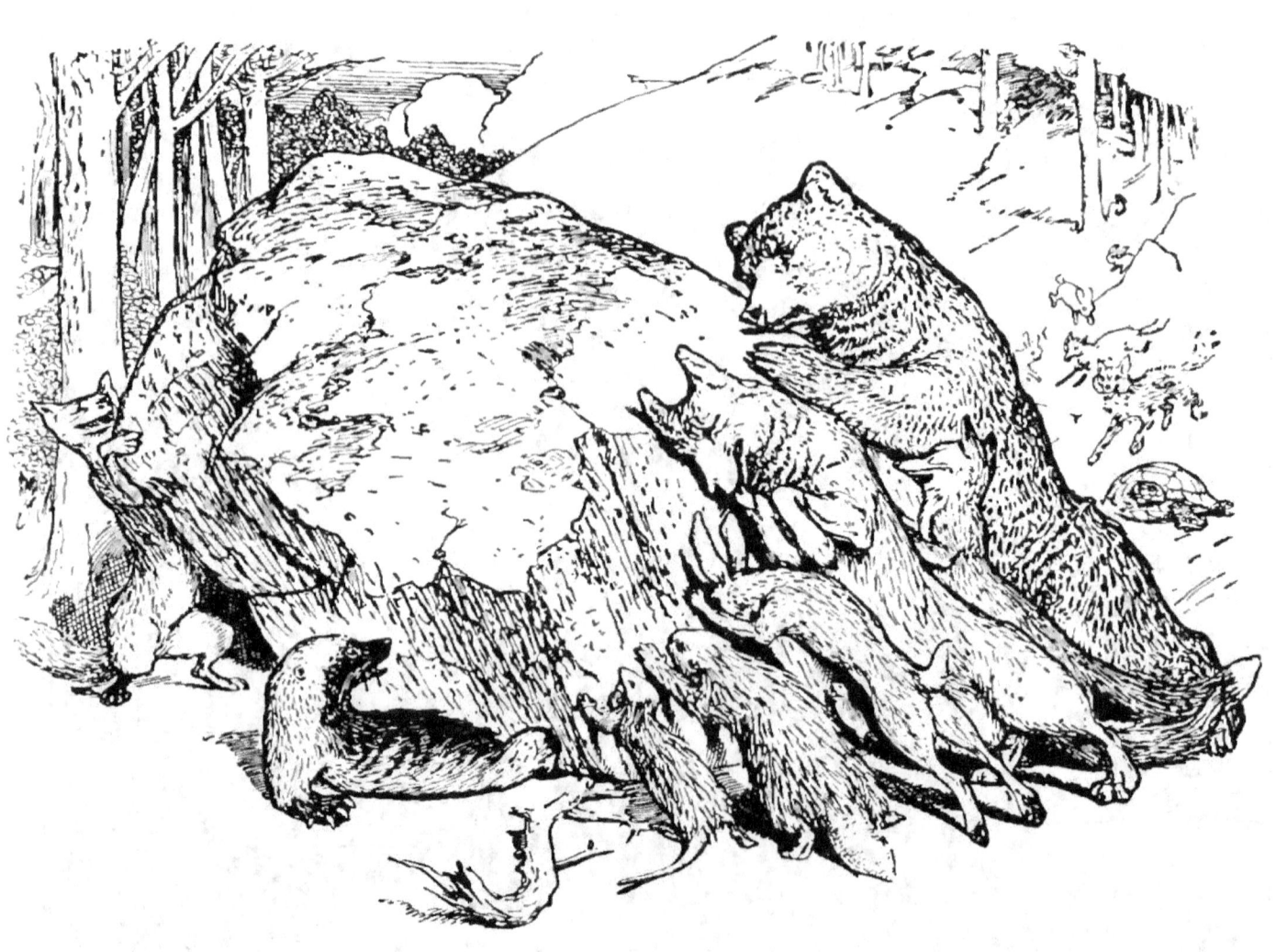

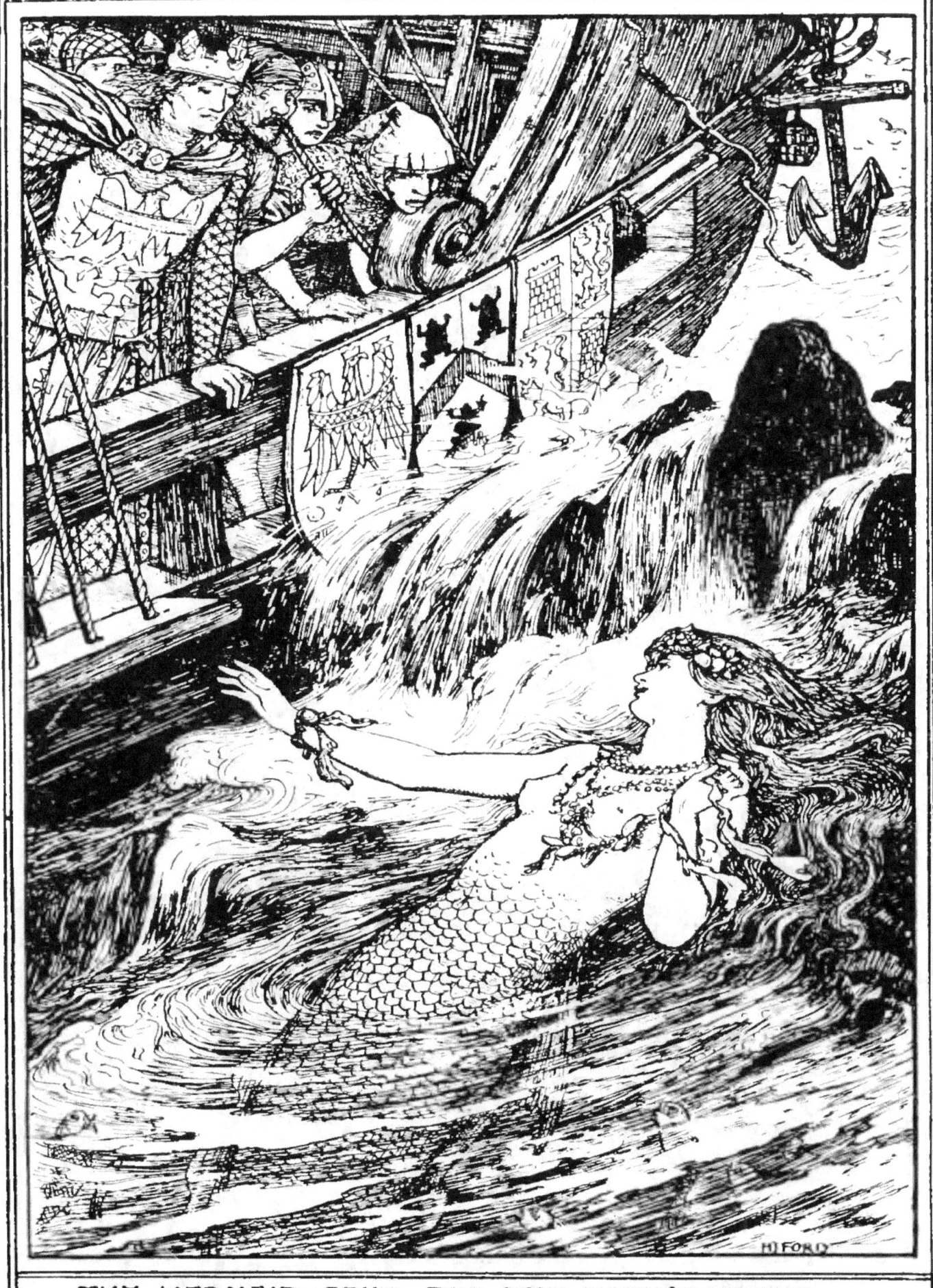

THE MERMAID ASKS FOR THE KING'S CHILD

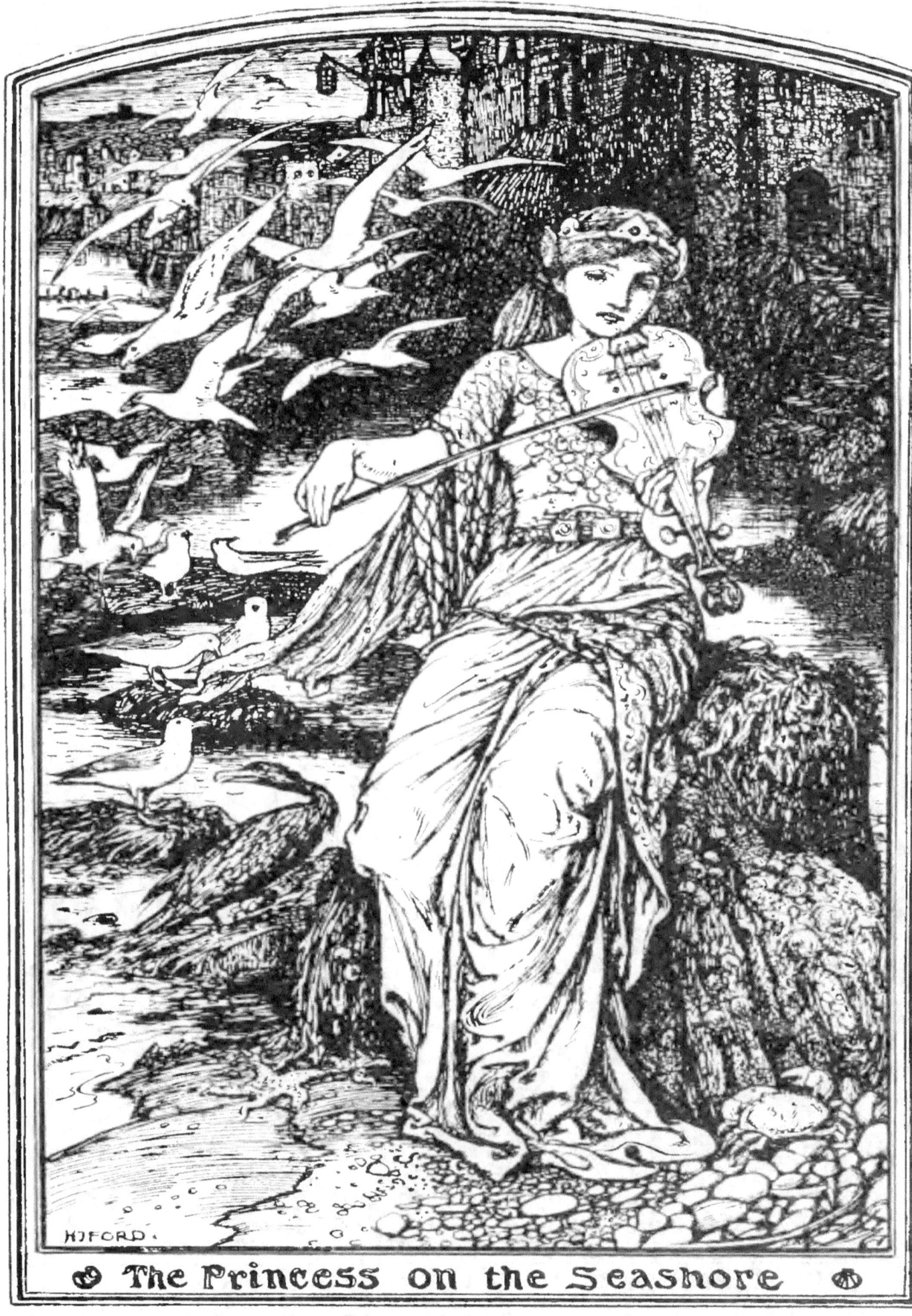

The Princess on the Seashore

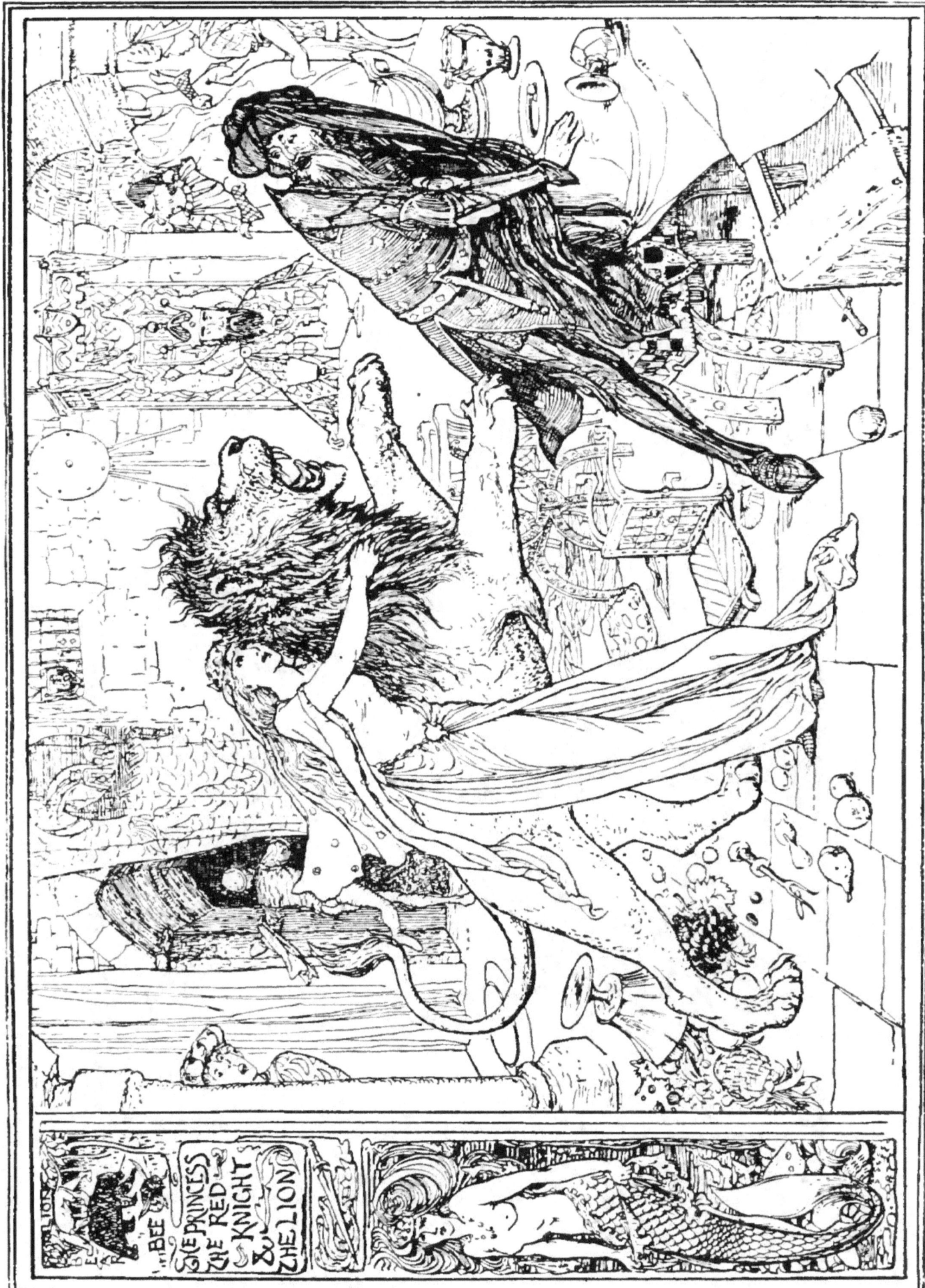

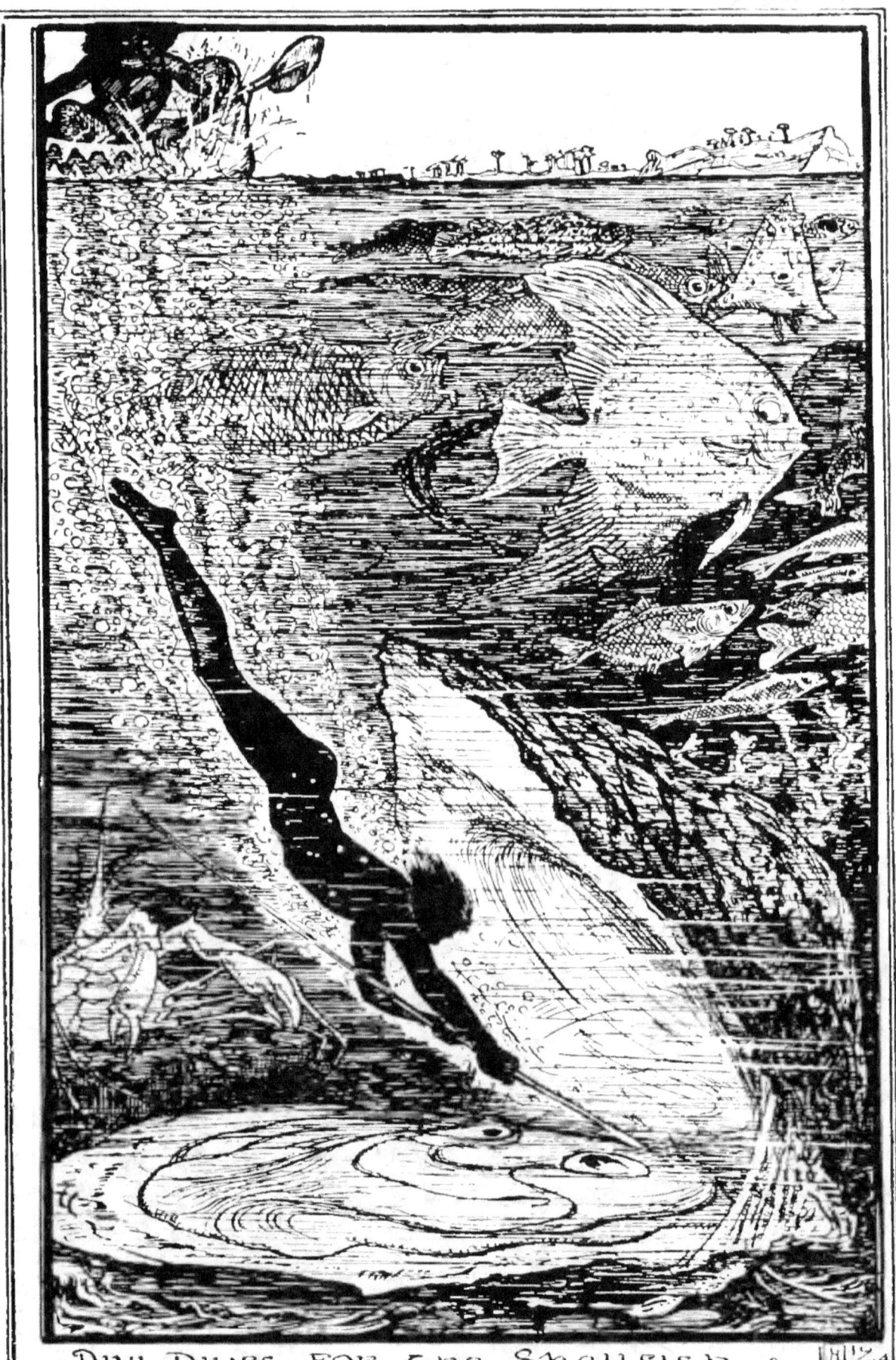
Pivi Dives for the Shellfish

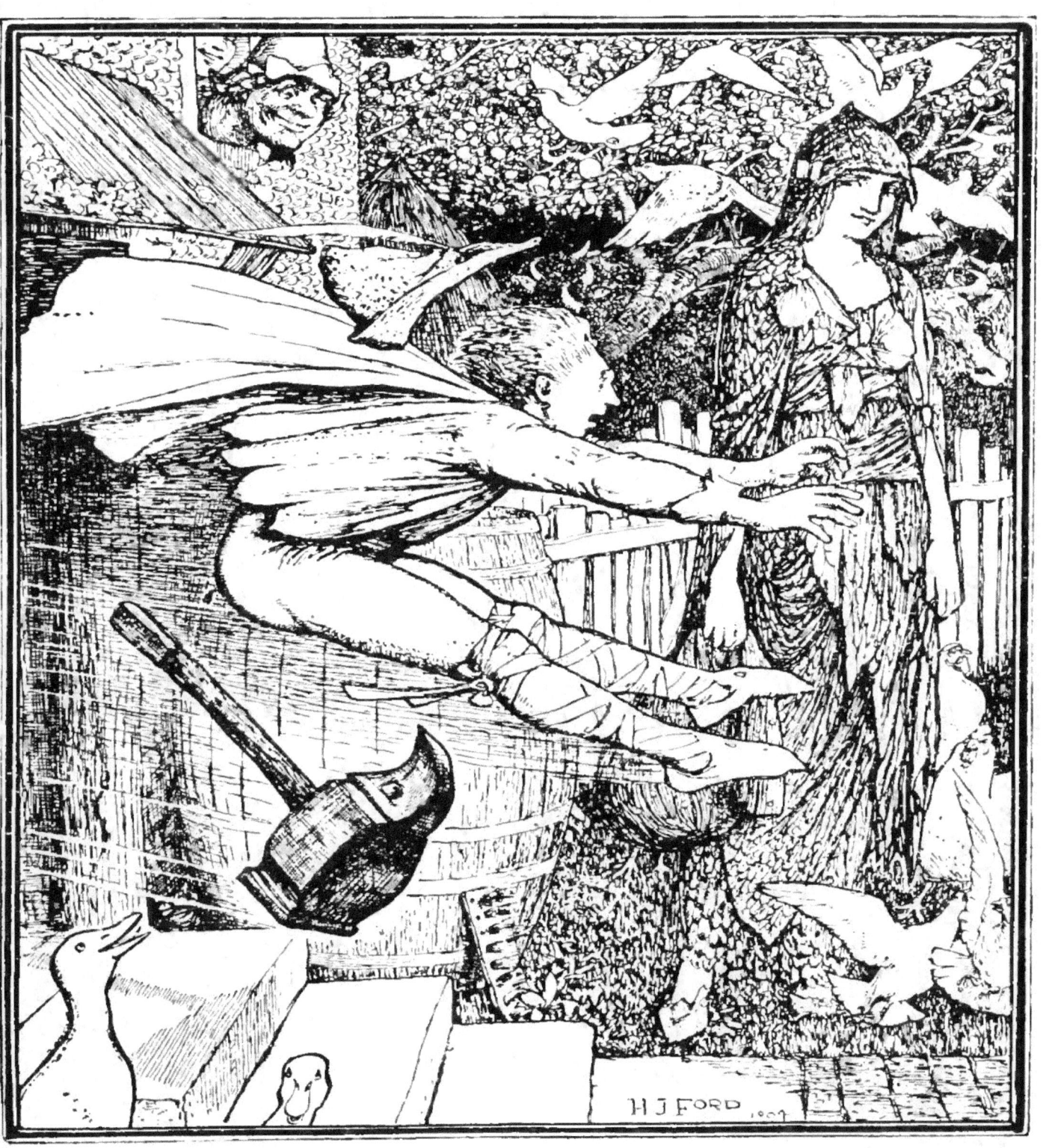

THE ELF MAIDEN'S HOUSE

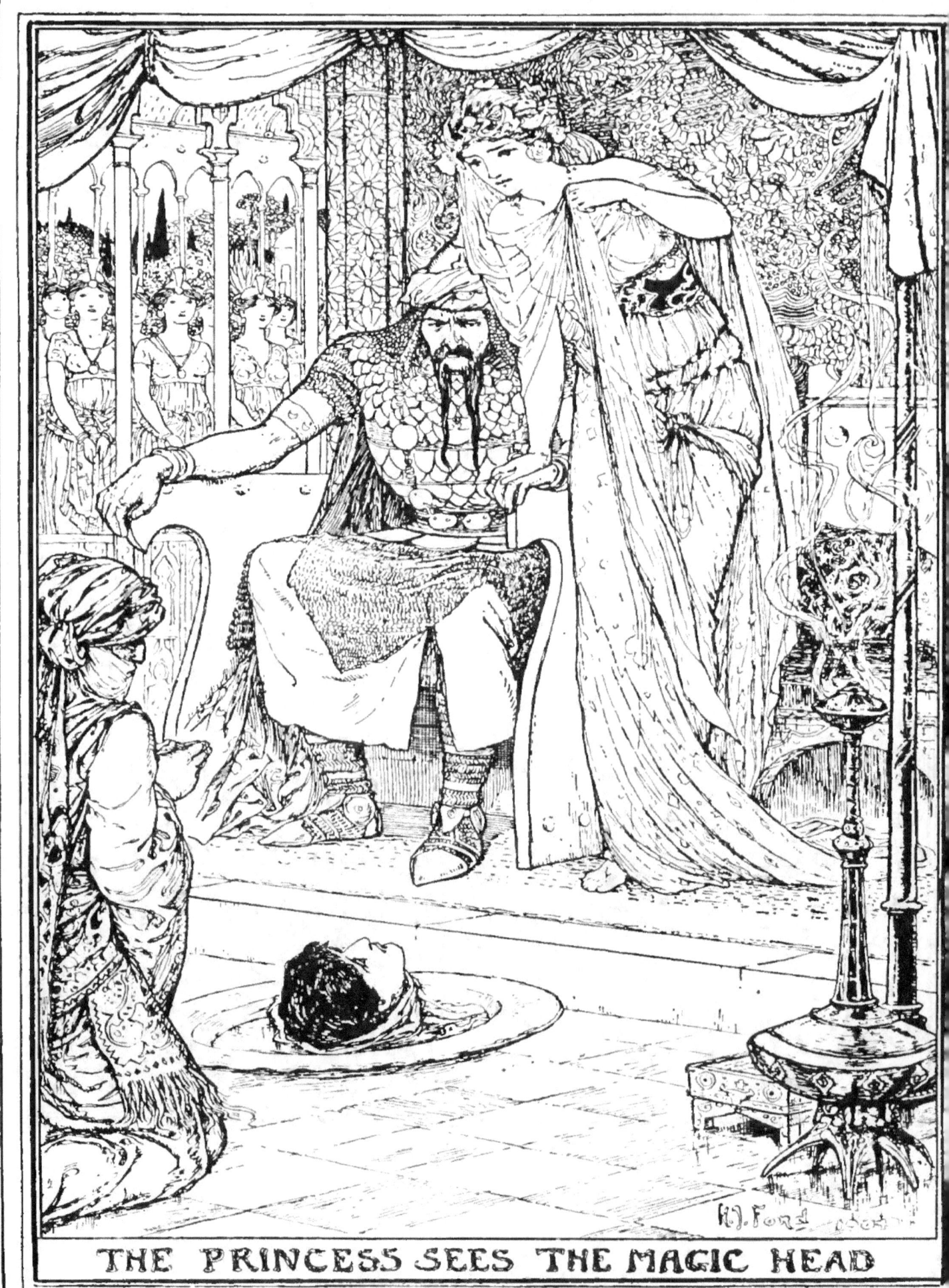

THE PRINCESS SEES THE MAGIC HEAD

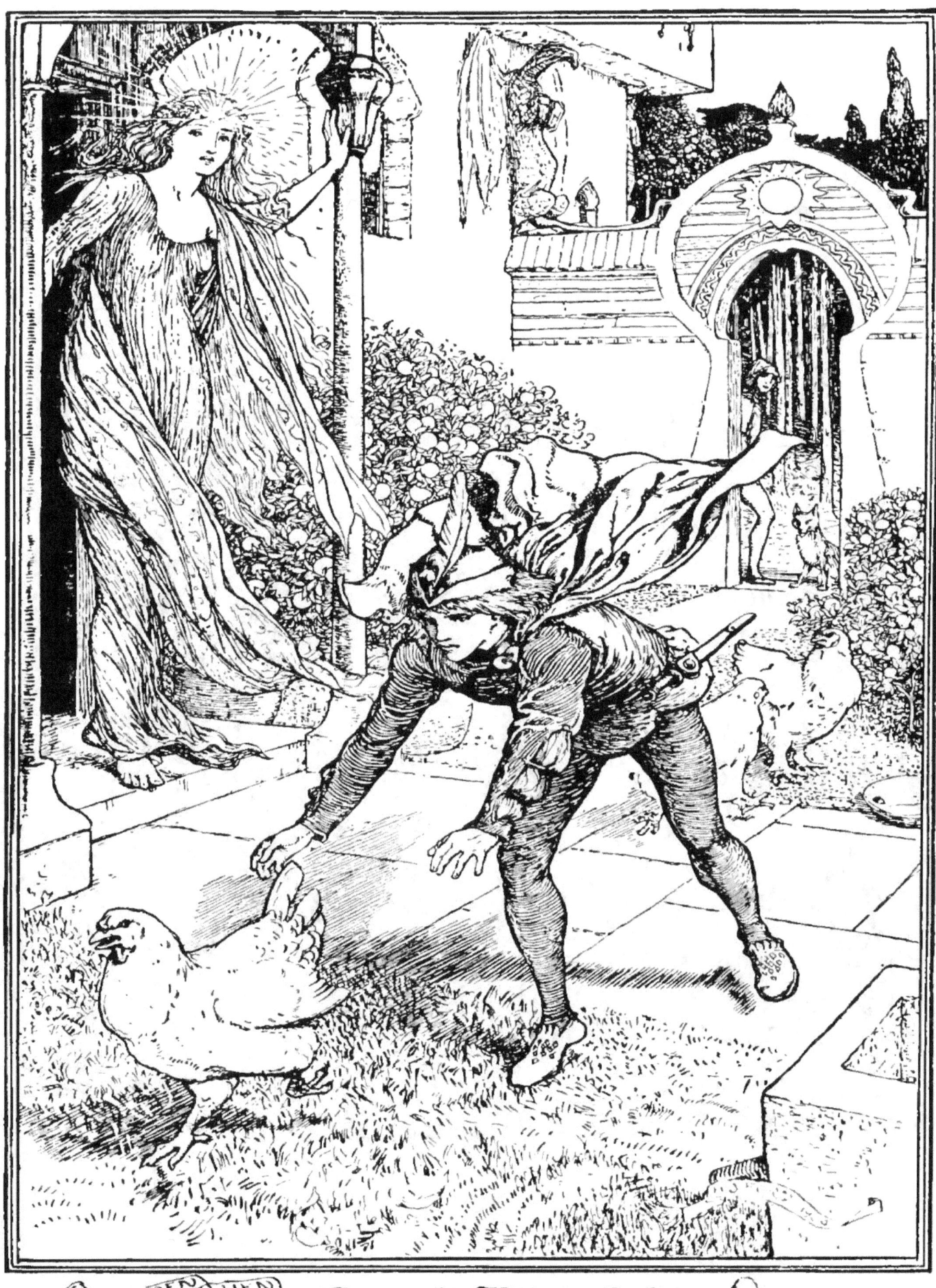
THE GOLDEN HEN WILL NOT BE CAUGHT NA NA

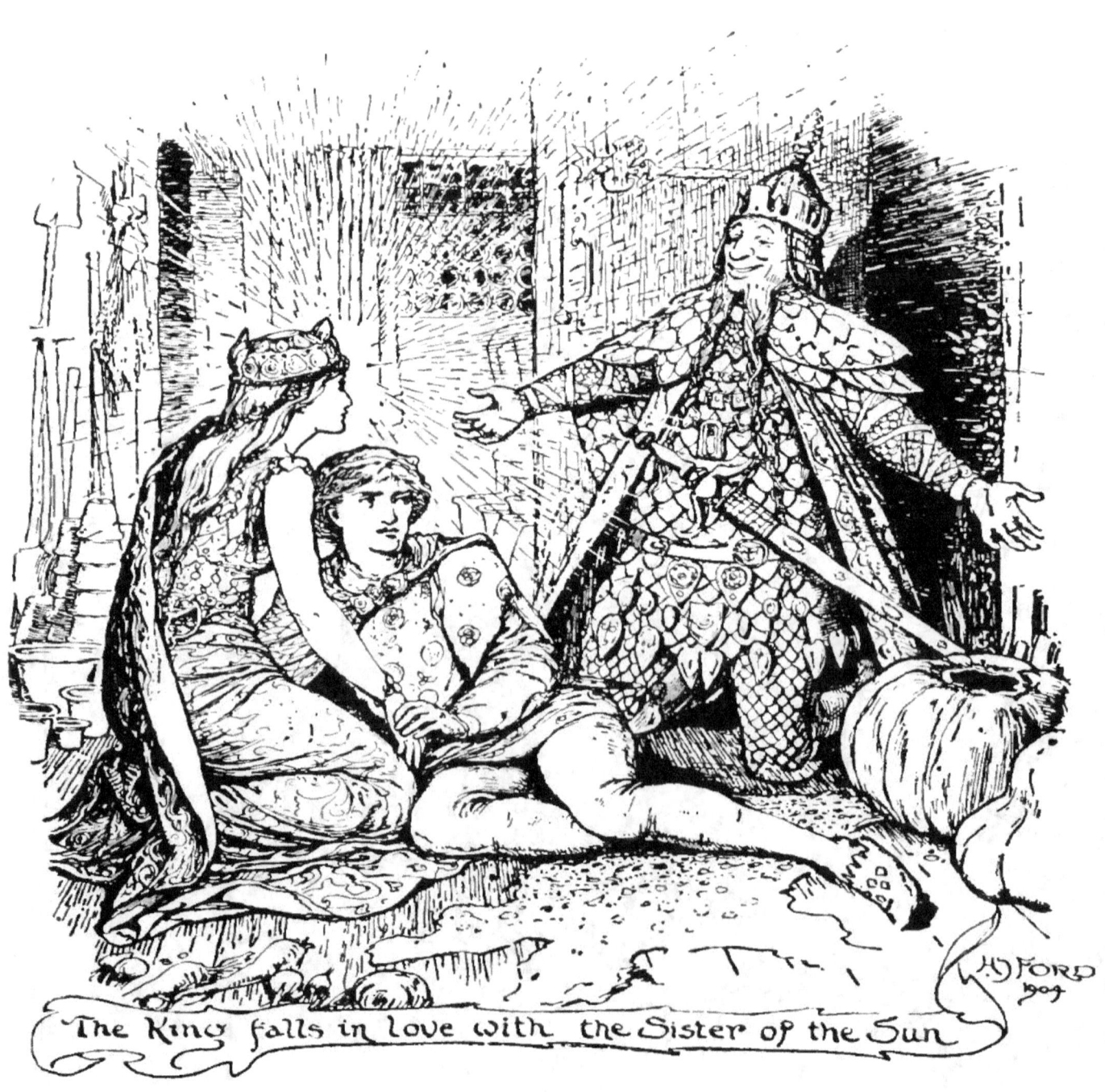
The King falls in love with the Sister of the Sun

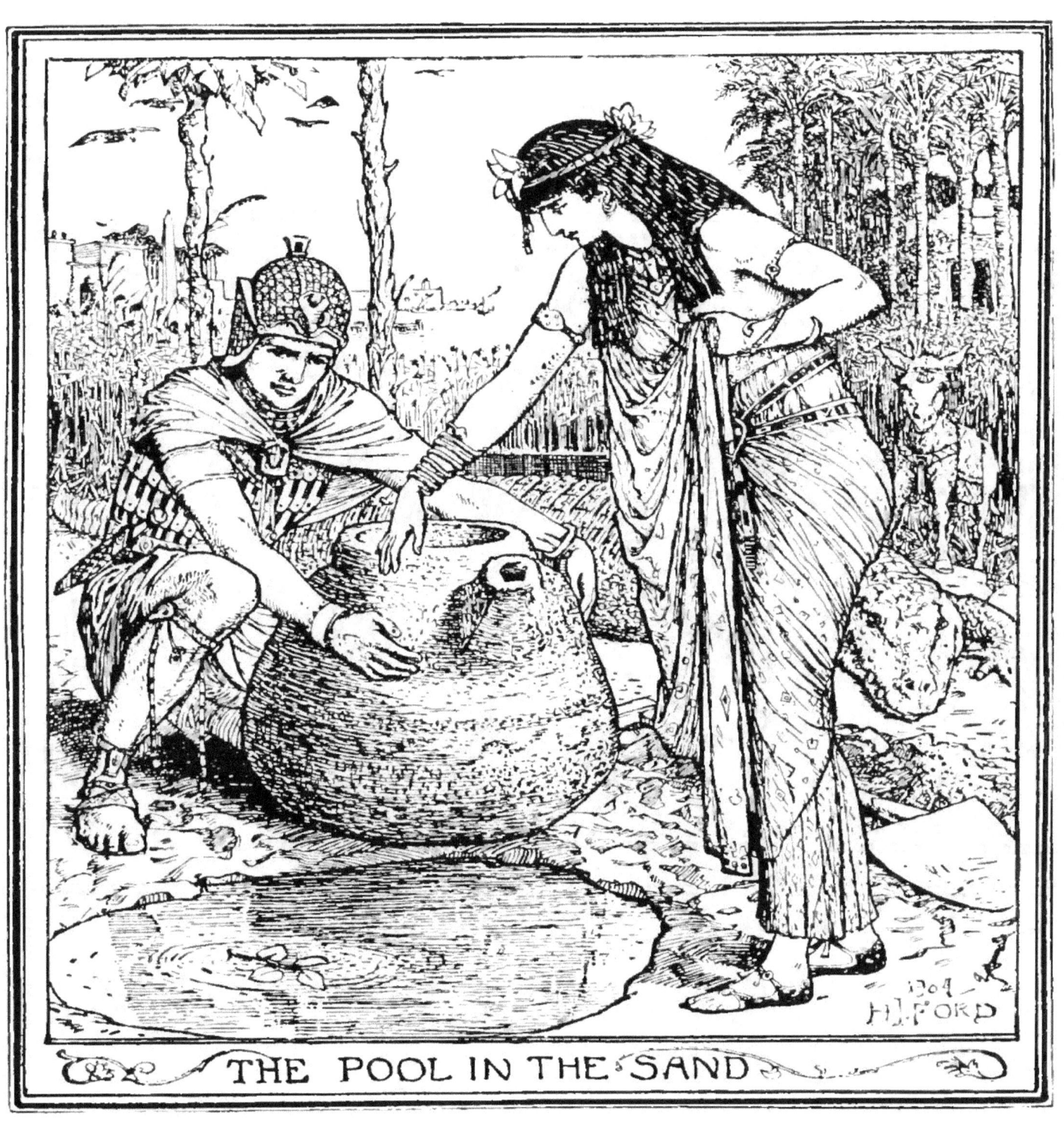

THE POOL IN THE SAND

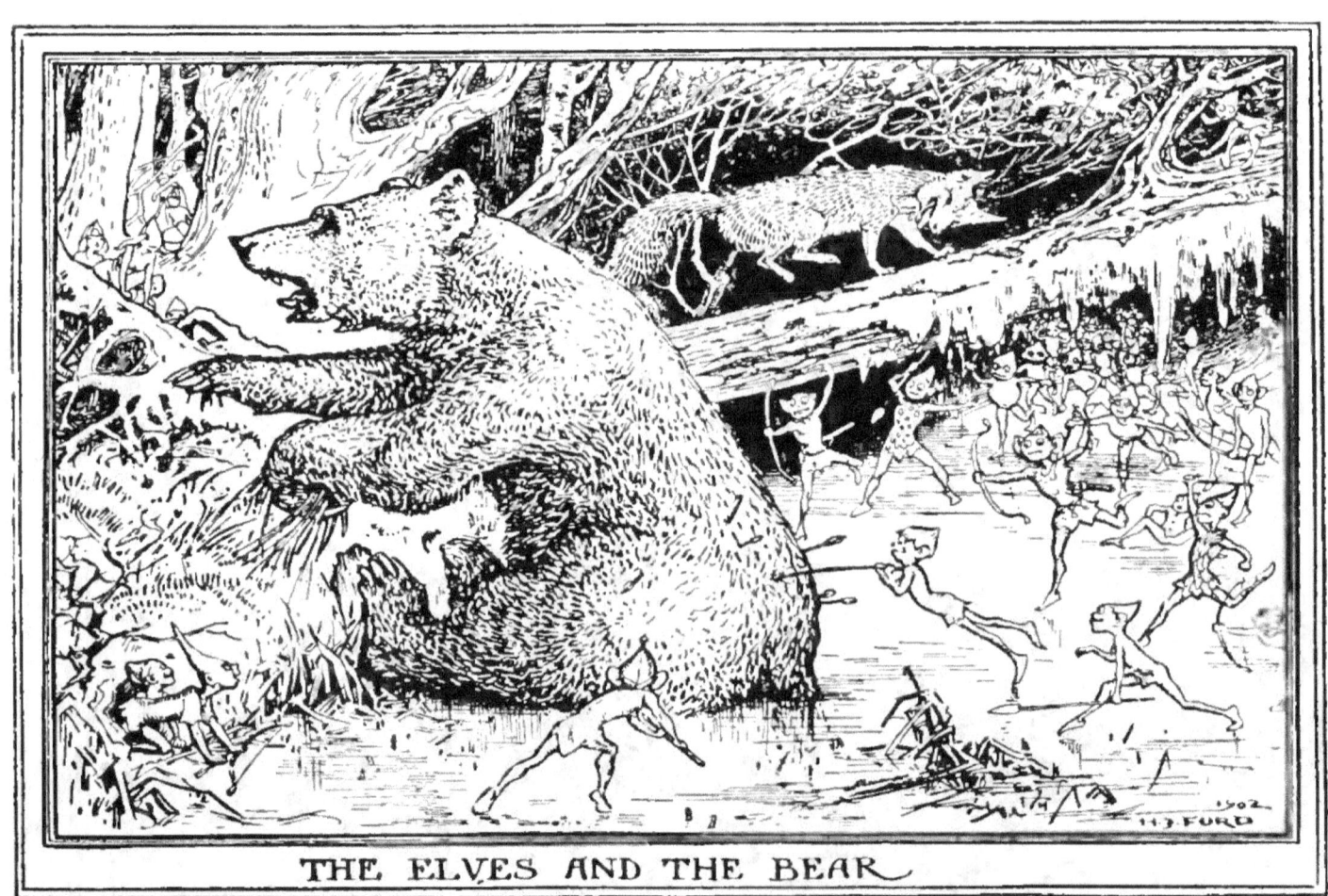

THE ELVES AND THE BEAR

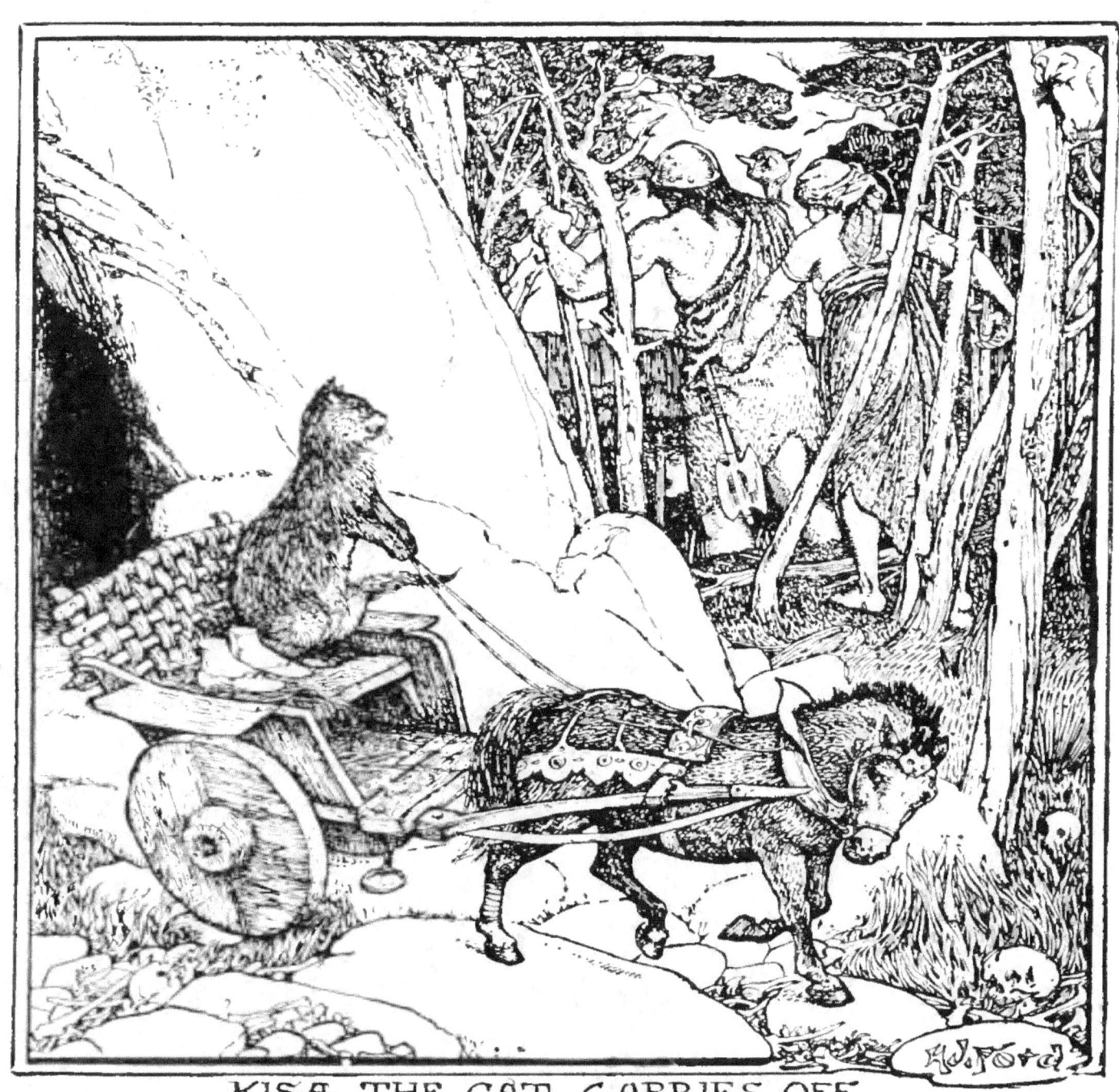

KISA THE CAT CARRIES OFF INGIBJORG'S FEET FROM THE GIANT'S CAVE

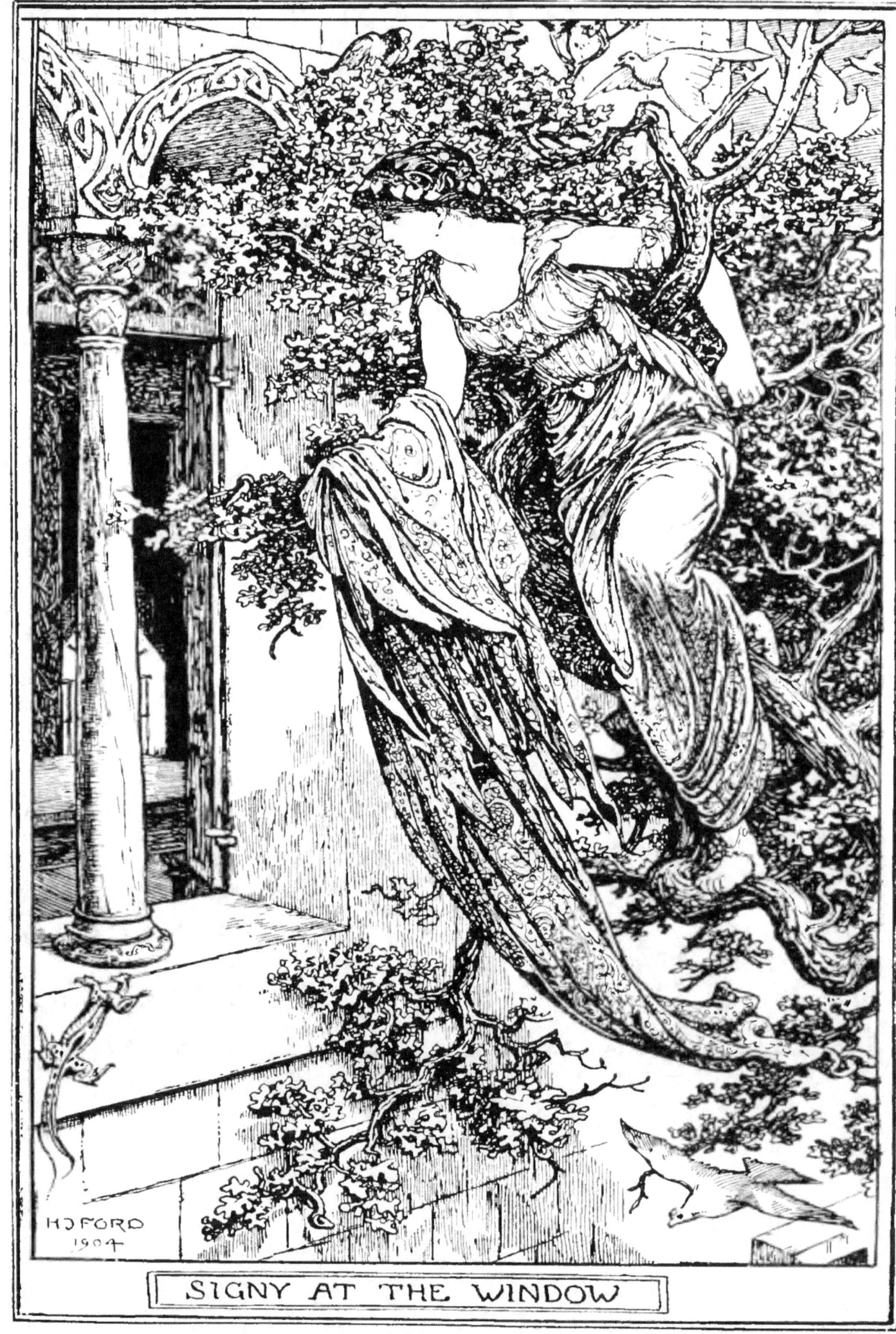
SIGNY AT THE WINDOW

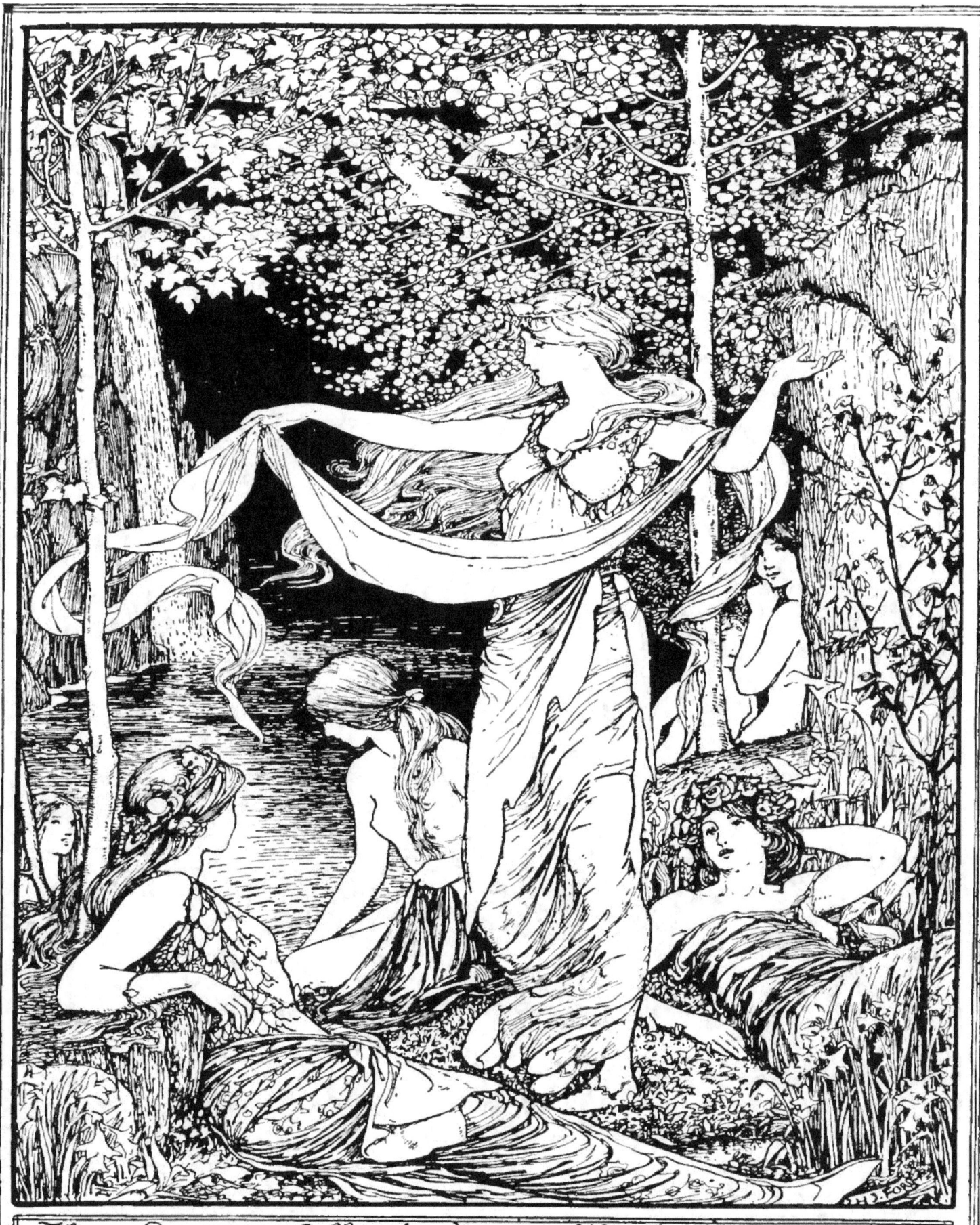
The Gnome falls in love with the Princess

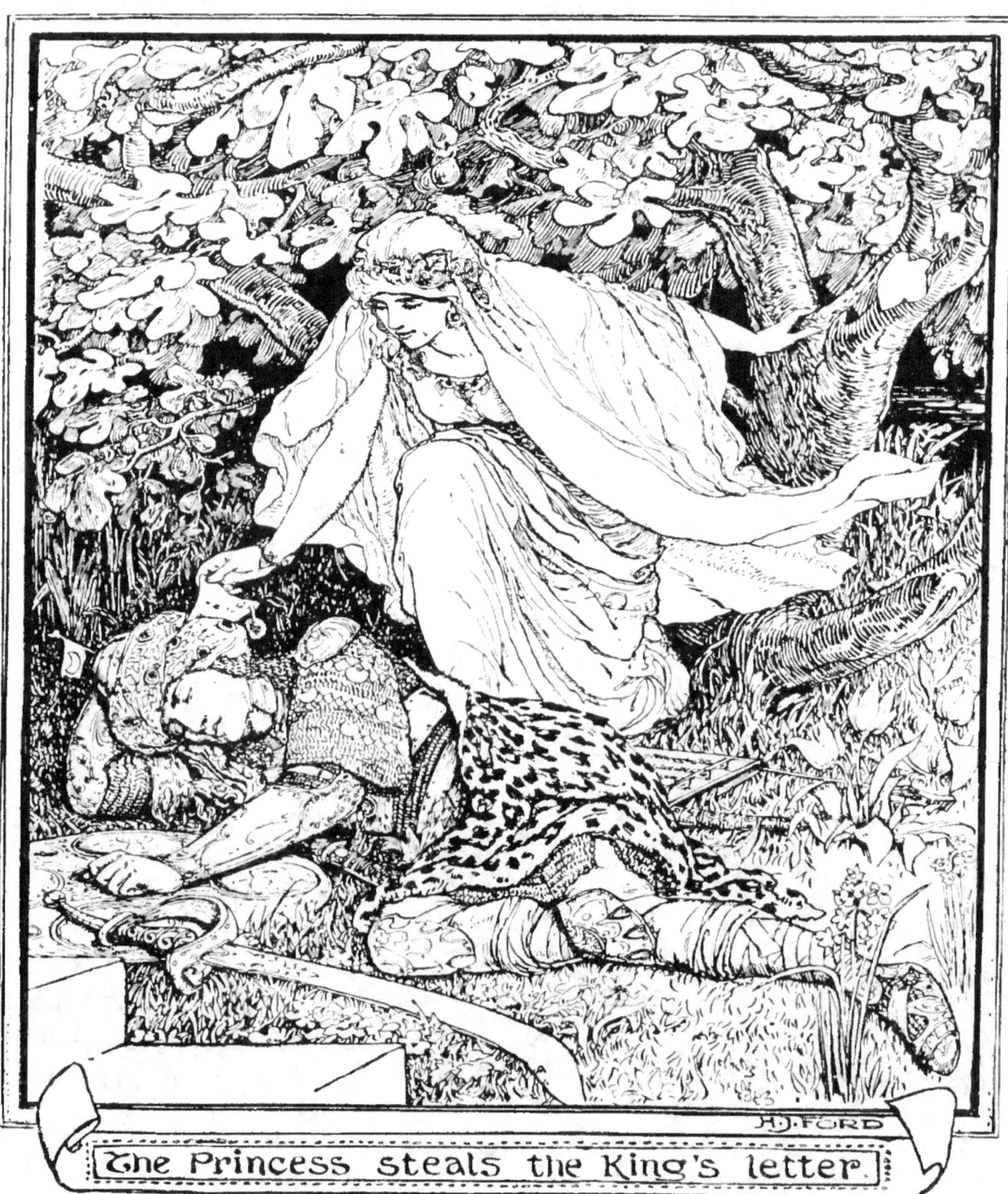
The Princess steals the King's letter.

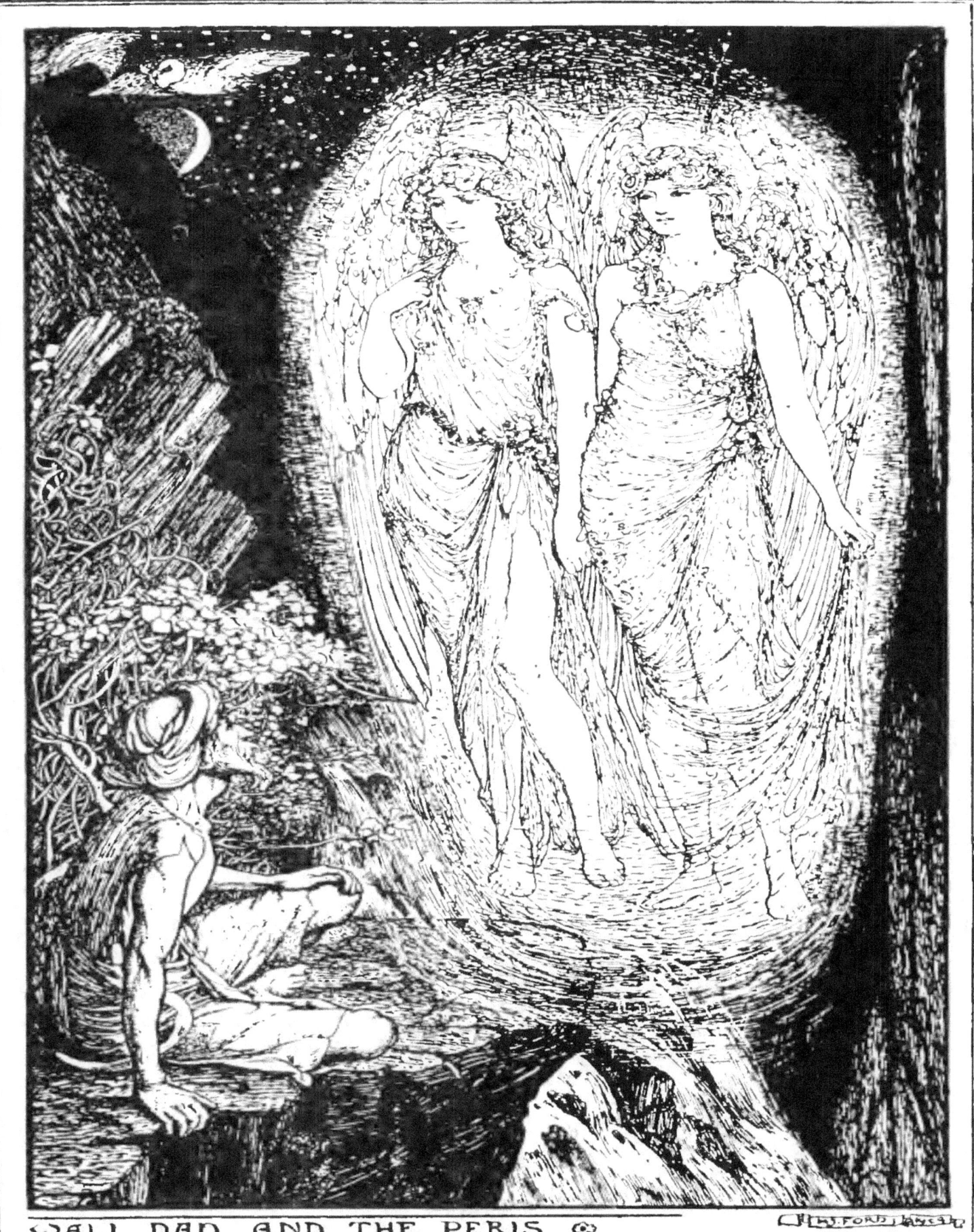
WALI DAD AND THE PERIS

www.ingramcontent.com/pod-product-compliance
Lightning Source LLC
Chambersburg PA
CBHW082223220526
45470CB00010B/3282